mz

9/2020

PATRIOTIC DISSENT

PATRIOTIC DISSENT

America in the Age of Endless War

Daniel A. Sjursen

Heyday, Berkeley, California

Library of Congress Cataloging-in-Publication Data

Names: Sjursen, Daniel A., author.
Title: Patriotic dissent : America in the age of endless war / Daniel A. Sjursen.
Other titles: America in the age of endless war
Description: Berkeley, California : Heyday, [2020] | Includes bibliographical references.
Identifiers: LCCN 2020017750 (print) | LCCN 2020017751 (ebook) | ISBN 9781597145145 (cloth) | ISBN 9781597145220 (ebook)
Subjects: LCSH: Sjursen, Daniel A. | War--Moral and ethical aspects--United States. | Military ethics--United States. | Dissenters--United States. | United States--Military policy. | United States--Armed Forces--Officers--Political activity. | United States--Armed Forces--Political activity. | Patriotism--United States.
Classification: LCC UA22 .S58 2020 (print) | LCC UA22 (ebook) | DDC 172/.420973--dc23
LC record available at https://lccn.loc.gov/2020017750
LC ebook record available at https://lccn.loc.gov/2020017751

Cover Design: Ashley Ingram
Interior Design/Typesetting: Ashley Ingram

Published by Heyday
P.O. Box 9145, Berkeley, California 94709
(510) 549-3564
heydaybooks.com

Printed in East Peoria, Illinois, by Versa Press, Inc.

10 9 8 7 6 5 4 3 2 1

To Mae and Joe "Bubsy" Peteley

Prologue

November 2006. Just south of Baghdad, Iraq.

It took me exactly one patrol to turn against the war in Iraq. To be more specific, it all unfolded on the first independent mission I led as a scout platoon leader assigned to the Third Squadron, Sixty-First Cavalry Regiment, of the storied Second Infantry Division. My beloved second platoon rolled out the gate of Camp Rustamiyah in southeast Baghdad that day in a single file of four HMMWV gun trucks on a basic "presence patrol": a vague, if ubiquitous, attempt to "show the flag" and exude a sense of security in a country then wracked by devastating sectarian civil war. There were nineteen of us in those inadequately armored vehicles. My seasoned veteran platoon sergeant was thirty-six years of age, the "daddy" of the platoon; none of the other troopers were older than twenty-eight. The average age was about twenty. I commanded, though I was all of twenty-three.

We turned right out of the gate and headed south, crossed the Diyala River, and proceeded along the aptly code-named Route "Wild." Matters deteriorated rather quickly. Halfway to the first of the populated villages—often labeled "suburbs" of Baghdad, though they bore little resemblance to the ones in New York's Westchester County that I envied from afar as a child in Staten Island—a small improvised explosive device (IED) prematurely exploded just meters in front of our lead vehicle. The insurgent "triggerman" had mistimed the detonation before fleeing. As always, we never saw or found him. Just as we'd been trained to do in the scrublands of Colorado and deserts of California, we halted, set a security cordon, and "exploited" the blast site: we took pictures of the crater, traced the "command" (detonation) wire, and checked the vehicles for damage. The whole affair lasted maybe fifteen minutes and was both terrifying and exhilarating. I'd—we'd—seen *combat*; we were warriors now! Oh, the stories we'd be able to tell in garrison town taverns when the deployment was over.

All of this and more crossed my mind. Still, I was an officer and had to think practically, too. There were so many questions: Who planted the bomb? Which sect, militia, or insurgent group did he belong to? Where did he run off to? Where did he or they store the bombs? How did the civilians know to avoid the (conspicuously empty) area? Were such attacks to be a regular feature of daily patrols? What if the blast hadn't missed? For most of these I had no answers, and neither the superior officers nor the leaders of the unit we'd replaced seemed to have any useful advice. What was certain was that someone, or some part of the Iraqi populace, hated us—enough to kill us. Even for a West Point–trained professional soldier, this was a profound and disturbing realization. Shit was about to get real.

So on we rolled southward towards the historic, ancient city of Salman Pak, once the capital of the ancient Seleucid (Greek) and Sassanid (Persian) empires. About a mile out I heard the distinct sound of gunshots in the distance, several pops in succession—pistol fire. Picking up the radio hand mic, I ordered the lead vehicle, immediately to my front, to pick up the pace and, in classic Indian Wars cavalry fashion, race to the "sound of the guns." What we found was a macabre reminder that the US Army occupied a nation locked in a brutal civil war. Two Iraqi teens were sprawled on the pavement. One's brains were leaking out; the other had a couple of holes in his upper chest. Somehow, both were still breathing. I yelled for my medic, and Doc, as we called him, rushed forward. Before Doc could get to the teen with the head wound—and because my own inexperience precluded my gaining control of the site and situation—the gathering crowd of locals tossed him into a makeshift ambulance, which proceeded to pull away without the other wounded kid. We'd later learn he died within minutes.

Our medic kneeled beside me over the teen with the chest wounds, but before he could render aid, Doc vomited and began to shake uncontrollably. In the many months that followed he'd prove a steady, competent medic and treat many of our own often seriously wounded troopers, but this was his first real-life victim. Almost immediately, another soldier, who'd been considered a screwup back at home station but also once worked as an EMT, stepped up and began treatment. It wouldn't be the last time this soon-to-be-decorated trooper saved the day with his medical know-how. Once the field dressing was applied, a few of my other guys loaded the quickly fading teen into the back of my HMMWV. Everyone mounted up, and we pulled a U-turn and sped back north.

I hadn't clearly thought through the next step, running as I was on instinct and adrenaline. I knew kids who toted pistols back home in my neighborhood of Staten Island, but for the most part these served as props for play gangsters. I'd never seen someone shot before, but I knew viscerally that the bloody mess in my backseat looked bad. Wounded local nationals—lifeless army code for Iraqi civilians—weren't technically supposed to be brought to or treated at US military base aid stations. But I'd studied the maps and I knew there weren't any operational civilian hospitals in the area, and none was closer than our forward operating base (FOB). And this kid wasn't going to make it without higher-level treatment—and fast.

So I made a few frantic radio calls to headquarters requesting an exception so I could drive the casualty through the gate and to the unit aid station. I received a series of denials, then equivocations, and finally silence. To hell with it, I thought—we're coming in! By now the gravely wounded teen was audibly wheezing. It was just about the most awful sound I'd ever heard. Past the gate we wound and screeched down the dusty base roads to the aid station, a rear-echelon sergeant—we pejoratively called such noncombat soldiers "FOBBITS" for being ensconced in the safety of forward operating bases, and in reference to the *Lord of the Rings* movies—screaming "Slow down!" at us along the way. After my truck came to a halt, I helped carry the victim up the ramp to the aid station. Within a minute the physician's assistant on duty pronounced the teen dead. So I walked out to the trucks, sat against my wheel, and shared a few cigarettes with my sergeants. There was blood on my hands, my fatigue blouse, even my belt. Then we loaded back up, on my insistence, and drove back to the scene of the crime. I found the father, broke the news, watched him cry, and accepted his gracious—staggeringly polite, without resentment—offer of tea.

It had been my first independent patrol. Welcome to Iraq. If only I knew that within a month such a mission wouldn't even be considered a tough one. Perhaps it's better I didn't. What exactly had unfolded that day, and what did it all mean? It turned out the dead teens had been cousins. To hustle a buck in an impoverished community within a larger collapsed national economy, they had engaged in the roadside sale of black-market gasoline by the gallon jug. They were Sunnis—one of the two warring sects of Islam—although, like many Iraqis, they weren't from a particularly religious family. On that particularly unlucky day, a carload of opposing Shia militiamen—themselves probably teens or young men—had pulled up, hopped out, and proceeded to open fire on the strangers simply because the targets were Sunni.

These small-scale gangland murders, on both sides of the divide, were remarkably common by November 2006, three and a half years into the American occupation of Iraq. My unit, which departed Fort Carson, Colorado, in October, had the misfortune of entering the war at the statistical height of sectarian strife. The young victims I'd discovered that day were just 2 of the 3,095 civilians in the bloodiest month of the bloodiest year of the entire war.[1]

I never felt the same about the mission at hand, the US Army, or my country in general after that day. It wasn't a clean break, so to speak, nor was it an immediate political sea change. Such matters are rarely so neat. Rather, it was perhaps the first of many waypoints on my own complex, nonlinear road to public antiwar dissent. Not all that long before, as a burgeoning neoconservative and George W. Bush admirer, I'd entered Iraq with some doubts about the viability and efficacy, if not the morality and legality, of the war. It wasn't going well, after all.

Though senior Bush administration officials had billed the

invasion and occupation as a "cakewalk"[2] that would "pay for itself,"[3] within scant months of the president's "Mission Accomplished"[4] announcement a Sunni-based nationalist insurgency broke out. The next year, Shia militiamen joined the fracas, and the Sunni side drifted increasingly towards sectarian Islamism, previously an almost unknown force in fiercely secular Iraqi society. Then in 2005, in response to the calculated bombing of Shia mosques, the civil war that the Sunni jihadis (soon to coalesce under the banner of Al Qaeda in Iraq) hoped for kicked off. The following year, the resultant maelstrom would reach its gruesome climax. It was into this seemingly apocalyptic chaos that my platoon drove on that fateful day in late November 2006.

Always an avid reader and follower of current events, I knew all this gruesome backstory as I boarded the off-brand charter plane to Kuwait, en route to Iraq, just a month earlier. It disturbed me. In fact, I'd read Thomas Ricks's then-popular bombshell critique of the Iraq War's lead-up and early years, *Fiasco*, over my two-week home leave just prior to deployment. I'd later learn that our squadron commander, the lieutenant colonel in charge of the five-hundred-man unit, had read the very same book at almost the exact same time. This too raised doubts in me about the prospects for victory in a war that was now mine to wage, and (more discomfiting) even the wisdom of invading Iraq in the first place. I knew, too, that US military casualties, particularly in and around Baghdad, were skyrocketing. The month we hit the ground, 111 American soldiers had been killed and nearly ten times that number wounded.[5] I wondered how this could be sustainable for an all-volunteer US military struggling even to meet recruiting goals in a war with no conceivable end in sight.

As I tossed and turned during the night after the patrol, I kept running the events of the day through my head. I couldn't shake all the questions and their fearsome implications long enough for anything but the most fitful sleep, despite knowing I had to rise early and do it all over again in the morning. This much seemed obvious: my unit—and thus my army and country—was clearly both voyeur and participant in a bloody ethno-religious civil war. We could expect to be attacked by one or both sides of that conflict, as well as to police and collect the refuse of the intercommunal bloodletting. The insurgency was multifaceted, the insurgents difficult to discern, and their tactics unconventional. Even if we could defeat (but what would that even *mean*, in practice?) one side of the bipolar insurgency, what of the other? And, if, somehow, we managed to miraculously suppress both sides, could we halt the civil war and secure the people in their respective communities? I knew for sure that none of us were really trained for that.

I was twenty-three years old, less than eighteen months past my West Point graduation. I was no defeatist, no liberal, no pacifist, and certainly no kind of dissenter. I still *wanted* to believe, with all my heart. I was proud of what I did, thrilled to put the uniform on each day; I adored my soldiers and truly thought what we did was special—to such an extent that the sentiment bordered on self-righteousness. Nevertheless, I couldn't shake the doubts that night, and everything I was to see in the days, weeks, and months ahead—in what would be unexpectedly extended into a fifteen-month tour—only added to those apprehensions. It was after witnessing my first fruitless murder, looking back, that I first indelibly knew the US military couldn't win in Iraq. That's as far as my skepticism went at the time. It would take the combination of these new on-the-ground experiences with my oldest love, books, to drive me towards outright opposition.

Every book, of course, has an author (or, as in the case of Donald Trump's bestseller, a ghostwriter[6]). But we authors can be a rather self-righteous and therefore suspect lot. One should always be skeptical when we explain what makes *our* particular work so timely and valuable. Perhaps the greatest sardonic social critic of my grandparents' generation noted at the very end of his life:

> There is a tragic flaw in our precious Constitution, and I don't know what can be done to fix it. This is it: Only nut cases want to be president. This was true even in high school. Only clearly disturbed people ran for class president.[7]

Well, maybe only wildly self-important people want—or think themselves interesting enough—to write a book. Count me as guilty as the rest of the literary crew. So here's a crack at why this one needed writing.

Americans today live in an age of vapid overadulation of their soldiers. They don't, the vast majority of them, want to actually *join* the army, the navy, the air force, the marine corps, or even the coast guard. That'd be hard, inconvenient, and, after decades of indeterminate wars, potentially dangerous! No, almost pathologically obsessively "thanking" service members and veterans serves three purposes. The first is a feeling of deep-seated obligation (maybe) to right the perceived wrong regarding how the last generation of troopers, from the Vietnam War, were treated. Mind you, serious scholars have long noted the significant exaggeration of the "spitting image" of Vietnam veteran treatment—the notion that most were literally spit on upon return.[8] Suffice it to say that while some troopers back then were undoubtedly disrespected—certainly at higher rates than this generation of veterans—large segments of society, usually majorities, supported not only the Vietnam War but also its participants until surprisingly late in the conflict.

That said, the second motivation for the often (though, admittedly, not always) vacuous gratitude is a sense of conscience-soothing embarrassment. Most Americans know full well that less than 1 percent of their fellow citizens serve on active duty and that they themselves chose *not* to do so. While by no means an accusatory slander, this is a simple, if uncomfortable, truth. Consider it a fact of life in a society that decided some fifty years ago to ditch its (usual) tradition of citizen-soldiering in times of large or extended wars and opted for an (ostensibly) all-volunteer, professionalized, standing military.[9] In such a culture as America's in the first decades of the twenty-first century, "thanking" veterans at sporting events, airports, or local chain restaurants feels—in the gut of the self-selected civilian—like the right or, at least, the requisite thing to do.

Finally, the societal veneer of what now truly amounts to soldier worship is driven by another salient factor: Americans have been *told to do so*. Remember what then-President George W. Bush told the nation's citizenry, soon after the 9/11 attacks and *just* as he unleashed the US military on an expansive series of ultimately forever wars—not that they must collectively sacrifice, or flood their local recruiting stations, but "get down to Disney World in Florida.... Take your families and enjoy life, the way we want it to be enjoyed."[10] The military only modestly grew in size over the ensuing years, and even when some two hundred thousand service members—most of them soldiers, some marines—were deployed to combat zones at the height of the Iraq and Afghanistan wars, income taxes were never raised, conscription was never considered, and instead the same professional "warriors" simply served tour after tour in harm's way.

This, what I've described, is what generally counts for "patriotism" these days: "thank" the troops, "love" America (or at least its gilded symbols), pay your historically modest[11] (despite the conservative hype) taxes, and—here's the key—keep your mouth shut. Nothing is being asked of you, materially or physically, so just politely champion the soldiers, wave a flag, and support the foreign policies of what's obviously—compared to those evil "terrorists" *over there*—a reasonably well-intentioned government. Only there's a catch: step outside those lines, take a rare interest in the nation's wars, and then, well, mister, get ready to reap the whirlwind. Expect pejorative labels like "hippie," "tree hugger," "un-American," "traitor," and/or the latest favorite: "Russian asset."[12]

That applies, ironically, even to the hyperadulated soldiers and veterans, of whom the prevailing culture demands near worship, if they dare open their mouths to tell something besides war stories (those are encouraged) and criticize or oppose the wars *they* fought. That's another problematic discipline buried in the fine print of the all-volunteer force concept: since military and combat service is a personal choice, even multitour veterans should expect to reap what they sow. Heck, this is fanatic personal-responsibility, up-by-the-bootstraps, capitalist America, right? Turn publicly antiwar and you're likely to hear the now ubiquitous retort: "Hey, quite complaining; you *volunteered*, remember?"

Thus, to me personally—and widely among my admittedly few

antiwar or anti-empire veteran colleagues—the expectation of pejorative slander has grown pervasively normal. In a strange twist, my experience has been that the character assassination, such as it is, comes more often from those who've *never* served than from fellow veterans or active troopers. Paradoxically, this is almost the inverse of that exaggerated spit-on-the-troops Vietnam veteran experience. At least in popular mythology, a civilian public turned on those veterans because they supported, tolerated, or chose not to avoid that conflict. Today's comparably paltry crowd of volunteer vet dissenters also tend to receive the worst attacks from civilians too, only this time for not being pro-war *enough*.

I am not simply some sort of self-styled victim as a result. Nor, rather importantly, am I alone in the experience of receiving such backlash. At most times during and after most wars in American history, sadly, dissidents—particularly veteran dissenters—have clocked in for plenty of public vitriol. It's partly human nature in times of war and especially when fearful—the tendency of any collective to rally together, submit to groupthink, and police (sometimes violently) the perceived threat of outlier opposition. Still, maybe because I've lived through these specific forever wars, something about the present moment feels especially dangerous and stifling. For in an age of corporate media, an overempowered presidency, increasingly sophisticated technological surveillance, and this nation's longest ever, seemingly indefinite wars, the demand for obedience to the current mores and norms regarding what constitutes patriotism has become equal parts more subtle and normalized. At least until one enters the venomous Thunderdome of the social media space.

With proportionately fewer citizens than ever serving in these forever wars, the popular foreign-policy apathy that shift engenders, and a government more apt and able to surveil and harass dissident thoughts and words, I fear that the contemporary—and, as I hope to demonstrate, totally unsatisfactory—narrow bounds of patriotism have the potential to permanently calcify. By no means will any solution to this structural problem I will identify be simple, nor will the key actors in the struggle to reframe patriotism as a participatory process—informed, foremost, by protection of America's aspirational republican values—come solely from within the military or veteran community.

This veritable crisis of our time demands big-tent, intersectional action from civilian and soldier alike. Only when the vast majority of citizens who have chosen not to serve recognize their inherent kinship with an increasingly insular, disconnected, and sometimes sententious post-9/11 veteran community will enough horsepower gather for the necessary mass demand—through the ballot box, street action, and media consumer choice—to be effective. Without prompt and widespread citizen action, this cult of vacuous patriotism constitutes, slowly but surely, an existential threat for the health of the republic. In the pages that follow, this middling but not so secretly idealistic soldier-officer will seek to explain why that is and what can be done to reframe *dissent*, against empire and endless war, as the truest form of patriotism.

1.

I was an exceedingly odd child. My parents were far from scholarly types (though my father was a lay history buff), and my neighborhood hardly produced any college graduates at the time. Nonetheless, I learned to read—and love it—at a very young age. The public library was my spiritual home, my oasis from a world of kids (even friends) I found generally boring from kindergarten on. I tore through the adult sections voraciously, especially history and foreign affairs, by the time I was seven. There used to be a rule that each customer could check out only seven books at a time, but soon the sweet, encouraging female librarians realized that rule wasn't designed for a kid like me. They learned my face and that of my mother and waived such arbitrary strictures for us. The summer before sixth grade, I read all forty books the local library had on Napoleon and the Napoleonic Wars. Such topical obsessions have never ceased to be a key part of my personality.

Always sort of a double kid, I spent my youth performing as one person with friends and in the neighborhood—cool, extroverted, a partier—and another in private, sequestered alone with my cherished books. This duality has never fully left me. During my army career, the paradox only morphed and reemerged. At work I played the physically fit, macho, lead-from-the-front, type-A combat arms officer rather deftly. At home or alone in my office, I'd consume volumes on the Middle East, military history, US foreign policy, Islam, and Arab culture. Just as reading and intelligence weren't valued by "popular" peers on Staten Island, scholarship and academic prowess weren't particularly lauded in the traditionally anti-intellectual US Army. To some extent they still aren't.

Before the deployment, I'd been busier than ever. The unit spent months, combined, in the field on training and maneuvers, and even office workdays regularly stretched to twelve hours. Add to that a young wife and the social necessity among junior lieutenants of hard-drinking party weekends, and suffice it to say, my usual reading load fell off. That all changed the minute we landed in Kuwait for a final two weeks of training and acclimation before moving into permanent quarters in Baghdad. What they don't tell you—and what necessarily (if unfortunately) isn't illustrated in action-packed Hollywood war movies—is that war is mostly boredom, punctuated by brief moments of sheer terror. Busy as the life of a scout platoon leader could be at the peak of the Iraq War, I quickly found that I had an inordinate amount of downtime. And so, as I always did throughout my youth, I filled my lonely hours with the love of my life: books.

I kept a count over those fifteen awful, life-altering months, fond as I'd always been of lists. As I recall, I read a total of 114 books, nearly all on the lead-up to the war, the history of Iraq, the theologies of Shia and Sunni Islam, and general regional studies. Additionally, my favorite interpreter, code name "Mark," actual name Akeel Ali Jasem, taught me conversational Baghdad-dialect Arabic for an hour or two a day. Over this extended period of immersive study, alternating with real-world combat and diplomatic experience in the ancient city, what struck me was just how much I didn't know that I didn't know. More disconcerting was how few of my peers or, especially, the squadron's more senior officers attempted—or cared—to learn even one-tenth of what I discovered. Ignorance, cultural obtuseness, I'd come to realize, was an American military trademark.

It turned out to be a brutal, ghastly deployment for my second platoon. Two soldiers were killed in combat; one killed himself while on leave, another after we returned home. Eight more were wounded, one paralyzed by a bullet through the spine. This was out of an original total of just nineteen scouts. Those lucky enough to emerge on the far end of the tour physically unscathed were all left riddled with post-traumatic stress disorder (PTSD), myself included. Then there was the horror that unfolded before the eyes of my soldiers: grisly corpses left in the streets from the previous nights' tit-for-tat sectarian shootings, the aftermaths of suicide car bombs, dead Americans from fellow units. It shocked the conscience and, for me, shook what remained of my religious faith. Though I still mumbled a Hail Mary to myself before each patrol—a guilty, superstitious leftover, I suppose, from a Catholic upbringing—I couldn't help but wonder how a loving, benevolent God could sit by while his creations *did* such horrid things to one another. I haven't regularly attended any sort of church since.

Over the course of the rather lengthy deployment, the days began to blur together. However, a grisly and almost absurd formula quickly emerged. Off I'd go on my daily patrols, often experiencing and observing vile events and increasingly living the utter futility of the mission. By mid-2007, after President George W. Bush defied the will of the American people—as expressed in the anti–Iraq War referendum-style midterm congressional election of November 2006—by increasing troop levels and appointing a new, enlightened, celebrity general, David Petraeus, reports (according to the new commander *himself*, of course) were that violence was down across the country.[13] Maybe it was true, or maybe the military cooked the stats. Either way, any drop in attacks and casualties would prove ephemeral, little more than a brief tactical pause. In September 2007 Petraeus told Congress, and Bush told America, that we were winning. This seemed curious indeed for those of us living on tiny rugged outposts ensconced in Baghdad. From *that* lens, "victory"—whatever that even meant anymore—seemed as distant and ill-defined as ever.

So I'd experience all this firsthand, viscerally, each day or night and then return to my olive-drab vinyl cot and crack open the relevant books. What I read, increasingly, was as disturbing and indicting as what I lived out on patrol. The real history of Western, especially American, involvement with modern Iraq, up to and including the 2003 invasion and occupation that I was then party to, revealed a stunning record of nefarious intent and action and almost farcical and Kafkaesque US policies towards the country.

Knowledge and experience, the twin necessities for enlightenment, combined to prosecute a near-flawless case against the Iraq War in my brain. It all seemed so obvious by the time my tour was done. How had I not seen it? How hadn't the ostensibly well-educated, highly informed elites in our government? And what of the people? Even if they (mercifully) hadn't had to live the war firsthand, as I did, all this knowledge was a matter of public record. Where was the collective outrage, the mass protest, the 1960s-style street activism? And what about within the military? Surely, intelligent, intellectually curious skeptics had to exist in the force, or at least on the West Point faculty. Was I the *only* one who "got it?" Rationally, I knew that wasn't literally true, but in Iraq, and especially after I left, I began to feel very alone in my knowledge, my analysis, my conclusions.

The horror, the futility, the *farce* of the war in Iraq was the turning point of my life. It was then, at twenty-four years of age, when I landed home in Colorado Springs, that I knew that war was at least built on lies, ill-advised, unwinnable, illegal, and immoral. This unexpected, undesired realization generated profound doubts in me about the course and nature of the entire American enterprise in the Greater Middle East—what was then unapologetically labeled the Global War on Terrorism (GWOT). Wasn't it absurd for a sovereign nation to declare war on a *tactic*? Furthermore, if the majority of regular Iraqi folks I'd met regretted, on some level, the departure of Saddam and agreed that life had been—as was empirically true—safer, less chaotic, under Baath Party rule, might the same be said about other US military enterprises in the region?

When I got in my then-wife's car just before midnight on December 31, 2007, and headed home from the welcome home ceremony held in the base gymnasium, American troops already occupied hundreds of military bases in dozens of countries. US soldiers killed, died, and propped up shaky local regimes from West Africa to Central Asia. Not a single one of those missions had, as of yet, succeeded, nor did victory seem close at hand in any one of them. For the most part, every US military adventure in this troubled expanse had been highly counterproductive. State Department statistics indicated, undeniably, that global terror attacks and the proliferation of Islamist rebel groups had both exponentially increased since American troops had begun to enter the region in full force.[14] In 2008 the Taliban was resurgent in Afghanistan, a country that Washington had largely ignored, first as a result of the Bush team's obsession with Iraq and then due to the utter collapse of security. After stewing over all this for a year or so, during which time I was promoted to captain, I entered my new unit, the Fourth Squadron, Fourth Cavalry, secretly opposed to the entire GWOT.

Still, I did my job, performed well, and remained loyal to the army or at least my own unit. My theory then was that "good" people needed to stay in the service, if for no other reason than to protect their subordinates, shield them as much as possible from the madness, and bring as many of these kids home from the next inevitable deployment. When I entered Kandahar Province, Afghanistan, in February 2011, I no longer believed in *anything* we were doing. I was there to do a job and to be as competent and empathetic a leader as possible—to play the white savior and salvage American lives. Also, having truly fallen for the people of Iraq, I hoped to treat local Afghans as well with respect and dignity in the process. The truth is I was by then simply a professional soldier—a mercenary, really—on a mandatory mission I couldn't avoid. Three more of my soldiers died, thirty-plus were wounded, including a triple amputee, and another overdosed on pain meds after our return.

If Iraq sowed these doubts and turned me, privately, against the wars, a particular moment in Afghanistan probably represented my breaking point, the pivot that led me almost inevitably to *public* dissent. One of my soldiers, a new kid I'd received just weeks before the deployment, had both legs blown off by a buried bomb and bled to death. Per tradition, I was obliged to give one of the speeches at his memorial ceremony at the squadron headquarters base. As I prepped my notes and as I delivered my remarks, it struck me that I hardly knew a thing about this young man. Perhaps that was a reflection of my increased rank and scope of responsibility, but I'm quite certain it was also a leadership failure on my part. In any case, I thought then and continue to wonder now, how in the world could I explain to his mother just what her son-turned-soldier had actually died for? I still haven't bothered to try. That's called cowardice.

A true man of principle, of courage, would have resigned immediately and joined the antiwar movement—such as it was at the time. What they don't tell you in vacuous, soldier-worshipping America is that almost anyone can brave gunfire and bombs. It's hard, terrifying, sure; but adrenaline and embarrassment keep most of us from outright cowardice in the face of the enemy. I did consider leaving the army, admittedly, but once again I hedged. I'd obsessively read my way through Afghanistan, to the tune of maybe seventy-five more books. I missed school, academia, professional learning—and I'd always dreamed that if I stayed in the army, I would return to teach history at West Point. So I applied for the rather competitive assignment while still in Kandahar. I made a deal with myself: get the position, stay in the service; get rejected, then resign. Deep down I probably knew I'd be accepted. And so I was.

The next stop was graduate school at the University of Kansas in the "People's Republic of Lawrence, Kansas," a progressive oasis in an intolerant, militarist sea of Republican red. It was the greatest assignment ever. I never had to don the uniform, I could grow some facial hair, and I received a full salary and benefits to do nothing more than focus on academics. There I studied American and military history, with a minor, of sorts, in imperial history. I read, skimmed, "gutted," as we called it, hundreds of books. It was during this stint in a scholarly state of bliss that I learned the necessary language and frameworks to ground my own doubts about and opposition to US foreign policy. The failures of the GWOT, it became clear, were just part of the tragedy of American global relations, a historical record of debacle and deceit. The United States was, from the first, an *imperial* enterprise, and I had been carrying water for that empire during my time in Iraq and Afghanistan. It all clicked, all seemed so manifest.

Why, then, didn't the average American see it, think it, believe it? Such things weren't taught in public school or in most college majors besides maybe history or international relations. The trick, for the owners of this country—the corporate tycoons, the media moguls, and the politicians they controlled—was how to *hide* an empire, how to convince the populace that their government's palpable imperium was anything but. That the US policy of global hegemony was a benevolent enterprise, the price of peace; that America was, as so many politicians repeatedly declared, "exceptional," an "indispensable nation."[15] This hoodwinking conspiracy required, demanded, a whitewashing of America's historical record: of native genocide, black slavery, the aggressive Mexican-American War, conquest and suppression of the Philippines, murderous campaigns in Vietnam and Southeast Asia, and now the counterproductive bloodletting in the Greater Middle East.

I had another epiphany. Part of the reason, I surmised, why so few Americans "got it" was that they lacked my combined experience of fruitless combat duty and scholastic training. After all, no one *reads* what these ivory tower academics wrote anyway. Professors have for decades eschewed their vital role as public historians and sequestered themselves in university departments writing increasingly esoteric (though important) tracts for one another's edification. I, again playing the savior, would remedy this. So, watching Senator Lindsey Graham (R-SC) on C-SPAN one morning as he railed against President Barack Obama's Iraq policies and ranted on about how the US military had all but won the war there, I absolutely lost it. After a few minutes of screaming and creatively cursing at the television, I retired to my bedroom with a laptop and wrote an angry letter. I had no idea what I'd do with it: was it an editorial, an article, actual correspondence for the senator?

Suffice it to say, I kept writing, and four months later I had ninety thousand words, a full, if accidental, book. The original letter morphed into its own chapter, titled "Shouting at Lindsey Graham." Once I realized my stream-of-consciousness rant had become a book project, I decided my monograph would be the one that bridged the gap between academic knowledge and accessible, experiential narrative. It would be the perfect book about war, at once memoir and policy analysis. Of course, I had no idea what I was doing. So, after googling, "How to publish a book?" I was lucky enough to find an agent and a medium-sized press, and I began to visualize my work on the shelf at Barnes & Noble.

Writing and publishing anything, a book or even just an article, while on active duty as a military officer is a tricky matter. The regulations stated that I must clear the entire monograph with the local public affairs officer (PAO) to ensure that, first, I'd revealed no classified information (I hadn't) and, second, I hadn't misrepresented the official policies of the US or been "contemptuous" of the president or any superior officer in my chain of command (this was more debatable).

Nonetheless, West Point's PAO was overworked, swamped with material to review, and basically told me to double-check my own work and bring any questionable sections to him for a quick review. The ease with which the book, titled *Ghost Riders of Baghdad: Soldiers, Civilians, and the Myth of the Surge*, passed the censors and gained "approval" was as remarkable as it was astonishing. Truth is, besides one full-bird colonel in the West Point Center for the Professional Military Ethic (CPME) who randomly called me to his office to tell me he hated the book and admonish me for being a poor leader in Iraq, there was almost no blowback. Of course, that's probably because hardly anyone bought the damn thing. My "perfect" book hardly made a splash. How naive I'd been.

The United States Military Academy (USMA) at West Point, many are surprised to hear, is, despite its many flaws, hardly an institution that simply indoctrinates automatons. It is a serious, if imperfect, academic body. Should one choose a liberal arts major and approach class seriously, West Point provides not just a free education but a remarkable one. I taught in the American history division of the Department of History, then under the enlightened stewardship of the respected Vietnam War scholar Colonel Gregory Daddis. Under his leadership, we instructors were coached to apply the up-to-date knowledge we received in graduate school, pursue continuing education, and teach our cadets according to the cutting-edge scholarly trends in civilian academia. He also gave us enormous independence, latitude, and room to experiment.

What also may surprise many Americans is how rarely he or other superiors in the department actually observed—or sought to control—my teaching. At most, I could expect a visitor to my classroom maybe twice per semester, out of a total of some 160 sections taught. So it was that I brought my own dissent, coupled with the prevailing frameworks and analyses of academia, into the classroom for the future officer students at the US Military Academy. It was the joy of my professional life. I taught them what a consensus of serious historians has long believed: that the English colonies and their successor, the United States of America, constituted a settler-colonial empire from the first, built on the displacement—by its very nature—and destruction of native peoples. The nation these cadets would soon serve was, at the very outset and still, defined by four core characteristics, original sins of sorts: racism, genocide, exploitative classism, and continental, followed by overseas, imperialism.

There was, as one might expect, some initial—and in some cases semester-long—pushback from the largely upper-middle-class, hyperpatriotic (in the traditional sense) cadets. That early skepticism, unsurprisingly, was strongest among the majority white male cadets, especially those from the South and Mountain West. Today's cadets are far more racially, religiously, and sexually diverse than at any time in the institution's history, even compared with my relatively recent tenure as a student (2001–2005). This has undoubtedly improved and widened the scope of social and scholastic discourse in the barracks and classroom alike. Still, cadets—and even more so the soldiers they'll someday lead—tend to be more conservative, rural, southern, and likely to come from a military family legacy than their civilian peers. Nonetheless, even I was pleasantly surprised by my ability to reach them, to elicit astute questions and cultivate critical thinking. By the end of each semester, I never ceased to be amazed by their collective progress towards intellectual curiosity, and their ability to thrive outside their philosophical comfort zones.

Nevertheless, I was always struck by the repeated queries throughout each semester from students both supportive and skeptical of my methods: Didn't I love America? Wasn't I a patriot? How could I *believe* these things (you know, facts . . .) and still serve in the US Army? To be fair, though these were simply constructed questions, they were important, all the more so because they forced me to interrogate my own thoughts on these matters and construct and communicate a cogent response, an alternative version of patriotism and "love" of country. However, in the process, I deduced—much to my dismay—that while I could and did successfully formulate answers to the first two queries, I no longer had an acceptable (for me, at least) riposte for the third. I'd reached the end of my by-then very frayed rope of continued—and justifiable—military service. In a sense, one could argue that those questions from my eighteen- and nineteen-year old students formed the genesis for this book, and for my soon-to-be extensive public dissent and eventual departure from the army. Not that I realized it then.

After my tour as a history instructor, feeling like I'd been pried out of my beloved office, I rotated (as 80 percent or so of the faculty do) back to the regular army. Next for me, since I'd been promoted to major, was an assignment at the Command and General Staff College (CGSC)—a year of continued professional education for all well-regarded mid-career professional officers—at Fort Leavenworth, Kansas. Sure, the army calls it a college, but after the fervent intellectual stimulation of graduate school and West Point and the raw excitement of daily teaching, the death-by-PowerPoint, checklist-based, formulaic, rote memorization of most learning at CGSC was a profound letdown. I was drowning, suffocating, in my own frustration, and my mental health deteriorated further than at any time since my initial return from Afghanistan.

I needed an outlet for the thoughts, doubts, and dissent swirling in my head. So I began to pen relatively short articles critical of US foreign policy over the last several decades, especially since the 9/11 attacks. I'd already published a book, but few had noticed, and getting outlets to print my soon-prolific pieces was a struggle. At first, I'd send my articles out to dozens of submissions email addresses for any and all publications, online or print, that I even remotely respected. I didn't hear back from anyone for months. Then Tom Engelhardt, a legendary editor formerly of Pantheon Books, reached out and—with significant editing and toning down—published my work at his own website, TomDispatch. The rest was history.

From that day in early 2017 until I medically retired on February 11, 2019, I wrote and published over 150 articles for dozens of publications. Sometimes I followed the regulations and ran the pieces by the base PAO; other times, mainly because his office couldn't keep up with my output, I didn't bother. I hardly cared any longer. I was too far down the path to dissent, too disgusted with the waste—in blood (ours and theirs) and treasure—of America's forever wars, especially in the wake of the election of Donald Trump as president, to play by the polite rules of the game. I just couldn't square the contradiction at the root of my experience. By day I'd take part in and often lead (the powers that be still thinking highly of me) mock planning sessions for executing wars with Iran on the soil of Azerbaijan, a place and scenario wherein *no one* bothered to meaningfully articulate America's vital interests. By night I'd read and write about the waste, counterproductivity, and impossibility of the US military's real-world wars in contexts as insane as our daily play sessions.

Most senior military leaders don't read critical analyses of US policy or, in many cases, read much at all. So I deftly flew under the radar for quite some time. My God, it was a lonely place, though. Being fervently and confidently antiwar and expressing as much publicly while still on active duty was often a gloomy state of being. I lost friends, confused confidants, and worried mentors. Mostly, I felt like a former monk who'd quit the faith and become an atheist while living in the monastery. Maybe, like so many guilt-ridden criminals, I was secretly hoping to get caught.

And so I was. Eventually, an anonymous, probably angry retiree snitched on me with a simple call to the Fort Leavenworth Inspector General's (IG) office. This set off a grueling, stressful, and scary four-month investigation, during which I was put on a no-publication order. I stood to lose my job, my pension, my benefits. No matter how much you sacrifice for the bureaucratic army beast and no matter how adulated you are by the citizenry, the institution will turn on you on a dime when you become an inconvenience, let alone a threat.

In any event, it all worked out. I was one of the lucky ones. Though the investigating officer eventually found me guilty of violating the regulation against publishing words "contemptuous of the President of the United States"—I'd (correctly) declared it was clear that nepotism was to be a defining feature of the Trump presidency—I received the minimum penalty: a verbal admonishment. Soon after, a bit too coincidentally, my team of mental health professionals determined that my PTSD and co-occurring diagnoses qualified me for an early medical retirement with full benefits at the rank of major. That was just dandy, as far as I was concerned. So the army and I parted ways in one of those highly unusual breakups. Better to quietly rid the army of my inconvenient presence on active duty without making too many waves. For that much, count me thankful.

In the year since, I've turned to a new, multi-hatted career as a professional activist: as an author, columnist, public speaker, and podcaster. I've lifted my voice, literally daily, against the empire for which I once and long dutifully carried water. Ironically and, I must add, quite rewardingly, I turned all that public speaking and leadership training and practice the army gave me against the war machine and its rich, powerful backers. In the process I've traded my identity as a soldier—the only identity I'd known in my adult life—for that of an antiwar, anti-imperialist social justice crusader. I've redefined my *dissent* as a truer patriotism, a love of country more deep and nuanced than the vacuous traditional definitions allow for.

I often wonder, looking back, with the Iraq War now almost thirteen years in the rearview mirror of remembrance, what seventeen-year-old me would think of my current work and life. My guess is he'd love hearing the first half of the pre-speech and post-article bios about my combat service, decorations, and rank achieved, yet hate the part where I turned antiwar and left the army in frustration. Then again, it doesn't really matter. That kid didn't know much of anything, no matter how ostensibly well read he was on the surface. Besides, none of us know the journey before us, the bumps in the road, or the experiential waypoints and pivot points in our lives. As such, it's hard to regret my choices, my extended military service—even if I am somewhat embarrassed by how long I stayed and the reasons why—for it made me the man I am today, a man I can finally say I'm not all that ashamed to look at in the mirror each morning.

Of this much, however, I am certain: my events-driven journey and fairly immersive, mostly self-taught academic education combined to complicate, forever, my own concept of patriotism in ways that seventeen-year-old me could neither fathom nor conceive. Nuance and complexity, slowly and then steadily, replaced both simplicity and certainty about what it means to call oneself—or live one's life as—a patriot.

The truth is, most Americans, myself included, possess a relatively deep conception of what patriotism means long before (if ever) they give the matter any real attention or, more rarely, develop any thoughts of their own on the subject. That's because, quite simply, their similarly indoctrinated parents—assisted by media messaging, government propaganda, and community social pressure—were imbued with a fairly coherent, if often shallow, construction of patriotism in their hearts and minds nearly from birth. Given that discomfiting reality, perhaps a brief, seemingly obvious, examination of existing definitions of patriotism—official and informal—is in order.

2.

Patriotism is one of those rather difficult words to define, to nail down in any agreed-upon way. It is also a word whose official—or at least dictionary—definition has changed over time. For example, Merriam-Webster now defines *patriotism* simply as "love for or devotion to one's country."[16] This seven-word explication of one of the more powerful forces in American and global life is striking in its very vagueness. Furthermore, this dictionary lists *nationalism* as a synonym for *patriotism.* This is as curious as it is potentially dangerous. A basic grasp of modern world history demonstrates the extraordinary differences between simple patriotism and the far more traditional chauvinism and superiority typically inherent in nationalism. After all, most serious historians agree that nationalism in the nineteenth and twentieth centuries, much like religious sectarianism in the eleventh to seventeenth centuries, was responsible for the preponderance and the bloodiest of European and global wars.

For the moment, however, let us allow the dictionary to speak for itself. It defines *nationalism* as "loyalty and devotion to a nation." *Loyalty*, as opposed to *love* for its definition of *patriotism.* These are not the same sentiments. Is it not possible to love something or someone yet, due to its or their bad behavior, not demonstrate blind or reflexive loyalty to that entity? For example, if I love the US Army but it adopts illegal and immoral torture as its official policy towards prisoners, might I not feel bound to loyally serve in that cause? Couldn't I conclude that true love for the institution demands that I adhere to its former, presumably authentic values? Indeed, since leaders of armies regularly change, to whom or what should the lover channel his or her loyalty? Perhaps love even dictates temporary *dis*loyalty while the loving soldier attempts to reform, reframe, or redefine—whether backwards or forwards—the values of the organization in question. Might not love sometimes trump loyalty or, at least, redefine it? And, while this discussion has thus far centered, theoretically (or perhaps not so), on the army, it stands to reason that the same could be said of the interconnection of love and loyalty to the country itself.

Furthermore, Merriam-Webster provides—contra its entry on patriotism—an extended definition for nationalism that raises further issues with labeling the two terms synonyms. Below its main definition for nationalism, the dictionary adds, "*especially*: a sense of national consciousness exalting one nation above all others and placing primary emphasis on promotion of its culture and interests as opposed to those of other nations or supranational groups." This, too, is rather different from a simple "love and devotion" to country. Rather, nationalism according to this construction—which is accurate, I think—implies an acclamation, almost lionization, of one's country *above* other sovereign states. What's more, as if to prove my point about the warlike perils of nationalism, the single example provided by the dictionary for the use of the term in a sentence is: "Intense *nationalism* was one of the causes of the war."

As I mentioned, the definitions of words evolve through the years and with the prevailing culture of the times. Consider that the first edition of Merriam-Webster's dictionary, in 1828, defined patriotism as "love of one's country; the passion which aims to serve one's country, either in defending it from invasion, or protecting its rights and maintaining its laws and institutions in vigor and purity. *Patriotism* is the characteristic of a good citizen, the noblest passion that animates a man in the character of a citizen."[17] This more complex entry for the term at hand does, as I see it, two things differently from the contemporary definition. First, we can see at the end of the passage that it clearly aligns patriotism with goodness, with "nobility," framing the sentiment as the utmost duty of a positivist citizen. At the same time, however, it expands and complicates the notion of patriotism by implying that this can be achieved not simply through physical protection of the country but also by preserving and safeguarding the "rights," "laws," and "institutions" of the state.

By this definition, from nearly two centuries ago, there is far more room for maneuver in one's personal take on patriotism. Everything hinges on how one interprets the nature of a country's guaranteed rights to the citizenry (in a democratic or parliamentary system like the US or Great Britain), the ever-evolving scope of written or common law, and the spirit of the state's institutions. Thus, in the United States, a self-styled nation of laws rather than rotating authority figures and leaders, which is constructed on a Constitution that delegates power to three presumably coequal institutions of government and which specifically annotates (originally ten) core rights of the citizenry, patriotism, by this original definition, has as much to do with "maintaining" the "vigor and purity" of those aspects of civil society as with defending (as a soldier does) the borders from invasion. Are we to understand that the modern simplification of patriotism to "love" and "devotion" to country encompasses these rather nuanced complexities? I for one would assert that this is so.

What, then, of *nationalism* by the standards of 1828? The term is certainly not listed as a synonym for *patriotism*, but then again, Merriam-Webster provides no synonyms or example contextual sentences in that bygone age. Rather instructively, the word *nationalism* doesn't appear at all. *Nationally*, *national*, *nationalize*, and *nationality* are included, but as a defined ideology of "national consciousness exalting one nation above all others," the concept doesn't yet exist. Indeed, this is a vital historical reality. Nationalism, as a philosophy, as a recorded sentiment—like most *-ism* words—is relatively new. According to the modern Merriam-Webster entry, the first recorded use of the term in the modern sense occurred in 1798.[18] Dictionary.com, however, dates the first use of the term to the 1830s to 1840s.

Remember, of course, that the nation-state as currently constructed and imagined is itself a relatively young concept. Before the mid- to late-eighteenth century, the vast majority of human beings lived under multinational imperial systems, dynastic near-feudal entities, or isolated provincial constructs. Loyalty or "devotion" was often divided between an absolute monarch, an imperial potentate, a feudal landlord, and family or clan leadership.

The state, as defined by strict borders, an ethnic, cultural, or political identity, and an organized bureaucratic structure that touched one's daily life, really only emerged between the seventeenth and twentieth centuries, depending on the country in question. Generally borderless islands, like Britain (with its shared parliamentary and legalistic tradition) and Japan (boasting a homogenous ethno-religious culture), may have made a relatively early and comparably seamless transition to nation-statehood, but continental entities such as Germany (not unified as a state until 1871) and the Austro-Hungarian Empire (which didn't fracture into somewhat ethnically distinct countries until after defeat in World War I) lagged further behind.

Furthermore, the successor states within the Ottoman Empire (which resisted final dismantlement until 1924) were largely Western inventions with suspiciously linear borders and often containing—for example, in Lebanon, Syria, and Iraq—decidedly multiethnic and sectarian diffusions. In these states, still some of the most unstable and violent in the modern world, the nature and place of the nation, nationalism, and the state itself remain highly contested. Much the same can be said of many postcolonial countries in Africa, the Middle East, and Central Asia. Just ask an American or Soviet soldier unlucky enough to have fought in Afghanistan.

In fact, it's unclear that the nation-state in its current form is necessarily here to stay or the preferred social and organizational construct of most or all people. To assume so is in itself a form of Eurocentrism or Western-centrism, the commonly held belief that because first Europe and then North America coalesced into such entities, this is the highest form of socio-structural development. Indeed, ISIS—no matter how ideologically abhorrent—represented a not altogether unpopular shift in the opposite direction. Their dream of a transnational, multiethnic, and potentially continent-spanning caliphate based on shared religious dogma constituted an outright rejection of the West-initiated nation-state model and, particularly, the postcolonial artificial states that the Europeans bequeathed to the people of the Middle East and that the United States has assiduously maintained. All of this must necessarily complicate any simple discussion of patriotism.

The point is that patriotism and nationalism are not the same thing and no official, mutually agreed-upon definition of patriotism exists today, nor did one in the past. This having, I hope, been demonstrated beyond a reasonable doubt, why, then, should the contemporary generation of Americans, in an age of endless war, accept the simplistic and constrictive bounds of patriotism as so often currently defined?

Like any standard irrational American male, I love sports. Watching the games, arguing strategies, and especially attending sporting events in person are all gravy to me, a well-needed distraction from the complexity, darkness, and absurdity of the "real" world. Add to that that as a notable extrovert, I enjoy being the center of attention, and one would expect me to enjoy what I'm about to describe.

Only I didn't. I'd developed into quite an adopted fan of the Kansas City Royals during my years in Kansas, as the baseball team's low-budget, small-ball, underdog persona struck a chord. Add the insanely cheap ticket prices—at least compared to those of my New York Yankees—and suffice it to say we watched a lot of baseball in Kauffman Stadium. So, back in graduate school, my then-wife secretly emailed a public affairs representative for the Royals. She sent pictures of me from my recent Afghan deployment, a short bio, and a description of my army career thus far.

She knew, as I did, that the Royals—and just about every other professional sports franchise by that time—honored one active or veteran service member at some point during each game. She also knew and appreciated, as a good thrifty New England Puritan, that the military honoree for the game received several free tickets in not-so-shabby seats. Sure enough, I was chosen. Much to my chagrin, my face and combat duty pictures were plastered across the jumbotron; a camera was pointed in my face, forcing me to awkwardly wave for far too long; my accomplishments were announced for tens of thousands of people; and finally I received a raucous standing ovation. No one *dared* keep their seats in such moments in the post-9/11 era: not in "conservative" Kansas City nor in "liberal" Boston. It just wasn't and isn't done.

Already decidedly antiwar, in the midst of penning a book critical of the Iraq invasion, and increasingly convinced that it was *actually* social workers, teachers, and nurses who belonged on the fields and jumbotrons of America's sporting rituals, I wasn't too pleased with the whole charade. Also, in an era in which there seemed little in the way of a large-scale, serious, organized antiwar movement and no military draft to ensure that average citizens had "skin in the game" of these wars, the whole thanks-via-applause aspect of the affair felt vapid, to say the least.

Yet it wasn't just that. The Royals, like every other damn sports team in the country, weren't satisfied—or secure enough—with one military recognition. No, first there had to be an embarrassingly gigantic American flag displayed and a military and/or police–first responder color guard during the pregame. Then, during the seventh-inning stretch, the crowd couldn't possibly just sing the traditional folksy ditty "Take Me Out to the Ballgame." Now it had become obligatory to follow that up with "God Bless America." The nationwide agreement on *this* particular national-pride song was especially curious. I never received a memo or a ballot beforehand; it just happened, seemingly overnight. The peculiar yet profound combination of presumed core religiosity and overt nationalism of the tune is striking.

Presumably, no one informed the commissioners and team owners of the sundry sports franchises of America that "One Nation Under God" wasn't slapped onto the end of the Pledge of Allegiance and "In God We Trust" wasn't printed on paper currency [19] until 1956 and 1957, respectively.[20] These (perhaps fashionably) late moves were, of course, made only in response to the perceived atheism of communism at the height of the Cold War, as a way to drum up nationalism, encourage unity, and differentiate the supposedly God-fearing United States from the evil, soulless heretics of the Soviet Union and Red China. My guess is the millionaires and billionaires atop the corporate athletics-industrial complex wouldn't have known or even cared that they didn't know such uncomfortable truths.

The definition of patriotism as constituting, for the vast majority of Americans (less than 0.5 percent of whom actually serve in the all-volunteer active duty military),[21] little more than the self-consciously public display—in a variety of ways—of "thanks" to veterans and, besides occasional first responders, *only* military veterans is an even newer phenomenon than the term *nationalism* itself. And its pervasiveness transcends the realm of sports. Repeated loudspeaker announcements in airport terminals express thanks and welcome to soldiers and veterans, and flight attendants also regularly encourage passengers to honor service members on the plane. Civilians load their bumpers with "Support Our Troops" and yellow-ribbon stickers.

And most of all, whenever an active-duty soldier or a veteran is outed to a stranger in passing, the conversation seemingly must stop long enough for the civilian to thank the soldier for their service.

This vacuous culture of "thanks" has truly gotten out of hand, hasn't it? Be honest. I'm just old enough to remember a time, before the 9/11 attacks, when honoring soldiers and veterans was mainly relegated to two main days of the year: Memorial Day and Veterans' Day. There were parades, war movie marathons on television, supportive newspaper editorials, and special events at sporting events on these two calendar dates. And you know what? That felt sufficient. It really did. Because taking this veritable soldier worship to the level society has in the twenty-first century can be perilous for the republic.

For decades and now more than ever, poll after poll has established that the *only* public institution that large majorities of Americans trust is the US military—not the presidency, the courts, or the media, and certainly not the Congress.[22] This simply isn't healthy—not for a democratic republic, at least. Maybe it would be appropriate for a tin-pot military dictatorship, but for an aspirational constitutional republic? Hardly.

Some of this gratuitous adulation is sincere and well-meaning. Certainly, no one wants to return to the (historically exaggerated, it must be said) bad old days of Vietnam when some antiwar protesters blamed the average troops, called them "baby killers," or ignored their trauma upon redeployment. Unfortunately, it doesn't serve the soldier or veteran particularly well. It doesn't change his or her life, doesn't stymie the record twenty-two veteran suicides a day or slow the pace of multiple deployments in indecisive and ill-defined wars for the active trooper.[23]

Nonetheless, many of us in the military and veteran community would gladly trade 90 percent of the inordinate thanks for an engaged citizenry concerned with and educated in foreign affairs. For the war machine, driven as it is by a profit-motivated military-industrial complex fronted by arms-dealing defense contractors, counts on—*requires*—collective public apathy. True, active citizens who read the global news daily think critically about America's role in the world and the prudence or prospects of US military operations: the war machine *doesn't want that.* Yet that's what this country's soldiers and veterans deserve. What they patently don't warrant is to be ignored between the thanks and the occasional check picked up by a kind soul at TGI Fridays, or to be shuffled around the Greater Middle East from one hopeless war to another by an unchecked president and an indifferent Congress like so many toy soldiers or chess pieces. Want to genuinely support America's veterans? Pay attention, watch how you vote, and create *fewer* of them.

Only that's not how most Americans think or act, not by a long shot. In the absence of a military draft, more than 99 percent of the population chooses to pass on military service. Unworried about the prospect of actually serving in one of the military's many wars—the armed forces are now fighting, dying, or assisting local militaries in combat in over twenty-five countries daily—and caught up in the standard struggle to earn a living wage, most citizens tune out foreign policy completely. Most of those engaged in politics at all, focus on the kitchen-table issues they perceive *do* affect them, such as healthcare, taxes, and social security.

If we're brutally honest, we'd admit that an embarrassing segment of even educated Americans couldn't pick out on an unlabeled map three of the seven countries the US bombs daily. Probably less than 1 percent could have both geographically identified and properly pronounced the name of the country of Niger, one of the more obscure deployment locales for the US military, where in 2017 four American soldiers were ambushed and killed by an Islamist militia that hadn't even existed in September 2001.[24] The takeaway is simple: in a post-draft, all-volunteer military in an age of endless war, the vast majority of the citizenry has divorced attentiveness to America's wars—or even basic knowledge about them—from their definition of patriotism.

So in 2020, nineteen years into America's longest period of continuous warfare, three basic conceptions of patriotism exist. The first two are prevalent, pervasive, and normative; the third appears to the untrained observer to be nearly extinct, or at least extremely rare and hidden from view, especially by the media.

THE FIRST, WHICH I'VE DESCRIBED IN DETAIL, IS WHAT I CALL "Pageantry Patriotism." Primarily focused on self-conscious public displays of gratitude and ceremonies, it sadly best matches modern American culture in this materialist, millennial age. This is the patriotism of flags, parades, anthems, pledges of allegiance, yellow ribbons, and vapid thanks. The beauty of it is that it is worn as a badge of honor, a point of pride, but requires *no* work, no critical thinking, no engagement with current events or inconvenient facts. It is a feeling, first and foremost. Patriotism is thereby simple, instinctual, reflexive. Pageant patriots exist on the traditional political left and right but in recent decades have mainly coalesced on the neoconservative, militarist right.

In this framework, pageant patriotism can also be combative. Pageant patriots take as a starting point not just that support for any and all American wars and support for the troops therein engaged are nearly synonymous, but that the former is actually requisite for the latter. Pageant patriots define their own patriotism as much by *opposition* to alleged nonpatriots as by any positive sense of what they are *for*. This has, in the past and even today, manifested itself through such pugnacious phrases as "America: Love It or Leave It!" Pageantry patriotism, much like the dictionary definition of nationalism discussed previously, is thus as much about "exalting" itself "above others."

As such, it serves as a cudgel for the self-styled patriot to wield against real or perceived ideological enemies, usually some imagined conglomeration of traitors, communists, hippies, Muslims, immigrants, and just basic liberals. These are the folks who were up-in-arms shocked by NFL quarterback Colin Kaepernick's decision to kneel in protest of racially charged police brutality during the playing of the national anthem. For them, another's remonstration—heck, even another's failure to cohere with the pageant patriot's preferred nationalist dogma—is judged a personal and public threat. In that sense, this is the most inherently insecure of all patriotisms.

The next most common contemporary construction of American patriotism is what I'll call "Passively Principled Patriotism." Most prevalent on the centrist political right and the establishment Democratic left, this version is often equally surface-level but less combative and usually tinged with at least some hint of (theoretical) complexity. These folks still either subscribe to or, in these intolerant times of endless war, have acquiesced to most of the dog-and-pony shows and obligatory thanks associated with pageantry patriotism, but they at least like to believe they support America and its troops *well*, because they do *good*. This is what the US is, or at least has been and should aspire again to be: a force for good in the world.

They, too, mainly accept at face value the modern "love" for and "devotion" to country in the most recent Merriam-Webster definition. Passive principled patriots, unlike the pure pageantry crowd, may not always support the government in power (especially if it is conservative Republican) or agree with the prudence of some of its particular wars, but for the most part they limit their opposition to muted complaints, ad hominem attacks on a particular political leader (Bush, Trump), and voting out that figure, all within the constraints of the established two-party system.

Passive patriots are fearful patriots. Often vaguely liberal, or embarrassingly centrist conservative, they're terrified of the ready pejorative attacks from pageantry patriots. They remember well, even if too young to have lived through it, the Cold War and the incessant slights brandished against those not deemed patriotic enough in the public political space: "un-American," "soft" on communism (note the sexual connotation), and "weak" on defense (note the masculinity connotation). "Never again" has been their mantra ever since. If necessary, they will out-patriot the pageantry patriots!

Thus, when 9/11 occurred and the "war on terror" began, they were all in, had stockpiled yellow ribbons, and were ready as could be to join the mandatory hyperadulation-of-the-troops culture. And when some of those wars (mainly Iraq) went bad and they either truly opposed them or saw a political opportunity in faux opposition, old-school, in-the-streets, Vietnam-era protest was out of the question. That would have been too risky, opened them to attack. No, the passive patriots play it safe, stay between the lines, and work, always work, *within* the existing system. For their sins, the troops and the republic have suffered mightily.

THE FINAL, LEAST COMMON FORM OF PATRIOTISM—AND THE one to which I unapologetically subscribe and that I hope to reframe for the mainstream—is what I call "Participatory Principled Patriotism" or, in times of dark necessity such as ours, "Patriotic Dissent."

It is a patriotism grounded in the more idealistic aspects of Noah Webster's 1828 definition, placing maintenance of America's aspirational values—"laws," "rights," and "institutions"—with vigor and purity over the easy, obvious requirement to defend one's country's borders. It is a patriotism that takes seriously the soldier's and officer's oath—which I proudly took upon each promotion during my career—to "support and defend" the *Constitution* of the United States. I served three presidents, in two separate wars, for a total of eighteen years—the great preponderance of my adult life. My loyalty to each was significant, to be sure, but ultimately ephemeral. My higher loyalty, by oath and by military tradition, was to the purported—if wildly imperfect—values of the American republican experiment.

Participatory patriotism isn't new; it has a long, proud history. Politicians, artists, and veterans alike have, across the centuries, pushed back when the majoritarian tide too often acquiesced to hegemonic and civil liberties–squelching phases in American foreign and domestic policy. President Abraham Lincoln, Mark Twain, and Marine Corps General

Smedley Butler (a two-time recipient of the Medal of Honor), as I'll soon demonstrate, personified this tradition. I and my many (though largely invisible) antiwar peers are but minor successors to these great men. When they saw their government, the representatives of their country, take the nation on the path of empire, domestic oppression, and values degradation, as we see now, they risked careers, reputations, and personal safety to defend the dream of the United States. Laying it all on the line: *that's* participatory principled patriotism.

Still, it *is* a dangerous path to embark upon. One's combat veteran status will not save him or her. Take the case of Hawaii Representative Tulsi Gabbard. A serving US Army major, Iraq War veteran, and Democratic presidential candidate for 2020, her unshakeable antiwar stance earned her exactly what? Vitriol and slander. And not just from social media trolls. Mainstream media pundits, serious national newspapers, and famous political figures (think Hillary Clinton) labeled her a "Russian asset," a "Vladimir Putin apologist," even un-American.[25] I've suffered the same attacks on a lesser scale.

As Martin Luther King Jr. observed in 1967, when he finally publicly opposed the Vietnam War, "dissent"—even today—is all too often equated with "disloyalty." Dissent always, but especially within the military, is a dangerous game. Far easier to subscribe to pageantry patriotism, or to hedge one's bet and be a vaguely liberal passive patriot. These are risk-free, consequence-free ways to live. They are also cowardly and detrimental to the dream of an inclusive, humble, example-setting America—what Abraham Lincoln called "a more perfect union."

Not too long ago, I received a snail-mail letter that listed my son's name, school, teacher, and address. It was a threat for my apparently unforgivable sin of opposing the American warfare state. I don't scare easy, but this note—seemingly written in lipstick—shook me to my core. In a certain sense, it defined these tragic times. No wonder most Americans hedge, or jump into pageantry patriotism with eyes closed and both feet forward. It is what we called at West Point the easy wrong over the hard right.

All of this is to say that popular conceptions of patriotism—at least in the current, post-9/11, forever-war, American setting—have lost their way. And it's hardly a partisan problem. Patriotism—whether expressed under Republican George W. Bush, Democrat Barack Obama, or whatever the heck Donald Trump is—has come to mean little more than "supporting" the nation's troops. Not only is this semantically problematic, but it also robs the term—and, more important, the powerful sentiment—of its weighty meaning and citizen obligations. As previously noted, in its 1828 conception patriotism not only was the highest duty of a citizen but also demanded that one maintain the vigor and purity of the rights, laws, and institutions of the country.

Since, apparently, the United States is an aspirational republic, even a model society, then, logically, patriotism would largely entail shepherding and protecting its democratic structures and values. In this more immersive, citizen-involved definition, thanking the troops and veterans would seem a rather minor aspect of the vital whole. This, then, raises questions about the role of loyalty and, conversely, dissent in the positivist practice of patriotism. If the government—and thus the policies—of a nation has gone off course, if its rights, laws, and institutions have lately been spurned, would not public dissent be the proper response? As Merriam-Webster originally framed it and as I've herein argued, couldn't opposition to one's government be considered the highest form of "love," "devotion" (the key words in the current dictionary definition), and "loyalty" to country? The answer seems obvious.

To a soldier then, or a veteran, can dissent be patriotic, and if so, how? On the surface, it seems unlikely. After all, military men and women work and live under a chain of command, in an institution that demands discipline and followership. If soldiers ignored every order they didn't like, the military would fall apart, lose all semblance of effectiveness. No one disputes this self-evident reality. However, there's another, rarely considered, more nuanced view of all this. And it is well that there is, because as Albert Maysles once poignantly warned, "Tyranny is the deliberate removal of nuance," and I'd argue that that is precisely what the vacuous veneer of pageantry patriotism—and the discipline it enforces—logically leads to: tyranny.

Remember that military officers swear their oath not to the particular president or government then in charge, nor to the flag or the current commanding general of the armed forces, but to "support and defend the Constitution of the United States, against all enemies, foreign and domestic." The *Constitution*! Sounds an awful lot like Merriam-Webster's 1828 definition, maintaining the vigor and purity of rights, laws, and institutions, no? What, after all, is the US Constitution if not a set of laws that defines the structure and practice of the republic's institution and, in amendments towards the end, delineates citizens' rights?

Thus, should the loyal and dutiful soldier's or veteran's government eschew the core, traditional values laid out in the Constitution—say, at a minimum, by waging congressionally unsanctioned wars—one could, as I would, cogently argue that dissent, in a variety of potential forms, would be the proper patriotic response. Luckily for the lonely, modern dissenter, there's a long and storied, though oft-repressed, tradition of dissent—particularly among combat veterans—in American history.

3.

I've seriously considered suicide. No, really. I'm not proud of that, but it remains an undeniable truth. There were years, not so long ago, when life just seemed hopeless, not worth living. PTSD manifests in a number of ways, and at my worst it translated into an inability to get out of bed and even look at my children, let alone function in polite, white, middle-class society (which I then largely abhorred and still do). There were times when I truly felt that I was worth more as a five-hundred-thousand-dollar US Army life insurance check than as a husband, son, father, and member of the human race.

There were, of course, various reasons for this. Depression is crippling; anxiety can drive one insane. Still, I think it was the loneliness of knowing I was right about the immoral and hopeless wars I'd fought, while feeling like I was the *only* one who got it, that nearly pushed me over the edge. It is hard to be right but alone. And, sure, I realize how arrogant that sounds, but history is near certain to prove me right. Hell, it essentially already has.

Precious few of my peers joined me in public dissent. I'd gain no solace from them. So, as always, salvation came from my books, from my literary soulmates. It was in the past, in history, in the volumes I devoured, that I found comfort and relief. I wasn't alone after all.

Rather, I was but the newest addition to the proud tradition of American dissenters, oft-forgotten but genuine participatory patriots who risked and too often sacrificed all for their dream of a nation that lived up to its promise, its hype, its aspirations. So it was that Lincoln, Twain, and Butler, among dozens of others, kept me alive in my darkest hour.

Dissent, of course, is multifaceted. It can be based on domestic concerns, and it often is. However, for the sake of this book I will focus on anti-imperialist, anti-stupid-war dissent. That's my expertise, academically and experientially. When Martin Luther King Jr. finally turned publicly against the Vietnam War in 1967, he identified three evils in American society: racism, militarism, and excessive materialism (hypercapitalism). When I taught at West Point, I focused on *four* traditional American sins: racism, (native) genocide, exploitative capitalism, and imperialism.

That said, to home in on the traditions of dissent regarding all three (as per MLK) or four (as per yours truly) evils of the United States would require perhaps a thousand pages. Besides, my own experience and expertise is in foreign policy, Middle Eastern history, and military history. So I will focus on the tradition of anti-imperialist, antiwar dissent. There's a long pantheon of dissent against American warfare and empire to draw from, and it's generally manifested itself according to four key strands of opposition. The excellent historian David Mayers coined the descriptive terms I will use.[26]

THE FIRST STRAND OF DISSENT IS THE PROPHETIC. IT INVOLVES strong religious overtones in which the dissenter critiques American policy as having strayed from the Puritan vision of the nation as a model society for the world to emulate—what John Winthrop in the seventeenth century referred to as a "city upon a hill." The prophetic tradition derives its core values and aspirations for the United States not from any particular human-crafted legalistic document, be it the Magna Carta or the Constitution, but from a higher power, usually the Christian God. Though the teachings and legacy of Jesus Christ have always been and remain contested, most prophetic dissenters employ his example in their criticisms of American foreign policy and, especially, empire.

Prophetic dissent characterized numerous famous figures and groups in US history. For example, many abolitionists who were against slavery and also generally against the Mexican-American War—a war of conquest waged on false pretenses—were devout Christians, often ministers and pastors. It is also important to remember that although they are now remembered fondly as heroes on the right side of history, in their day the abolitionists were *hated*, small in number, and largely considered fringe, radical kooks.

Another prophetic dissenter was the three-time presidential contender and secretary of state under Woodrow Wilson, William Jennings Bryan. A brilliant orator, Bryan regularly peppered his speeches—his most famous was the Cross of Gold speech—with religious, Christological imagery.[27] A strong opponent, at the turn of the century, of American imperialism, specifically the seizure and suppression of the Philippines, he regularly framed his dissent so as to pit contemporary US empire against the values of Christ himself.

Martin Luther King Jr., popularly remembered (and sanitized[28]) as a polite, inclusive civil rights activist, was profoundly radical for both his times and, frankly, our own. By the end of his young life and career—he was just thirty-nine when he was assassinated—King had expanded his rhetoric and work to challenge American capitalism and war making, which he called "excessive materialism" and "militarism." King, of course, like many mid-twentieth-century civil rights leaders and activists, was a devoutly religious man and couched his arguments in biblical values. He was first and foremost a reverend, classically trained in theology. In 1967, when King took the highly risky step of publicly denouncing the ongoing war in his "Beyond Vietnam" speech, he delivered his remarks at Riverside Church in New York City.

Early in the speech, King nodded towards the importance of its setting and the vital role of Christians in opposing an immoral war. He stated, "I come to this magnificent house of worship tonight because my conscience leaves me no other choice," and "We must rejoice as well, for surely this is the first time in our nation's history that a significant number of its religious leaders have chosen to move beyond the prophesying of smooth patriotism to the high grounds of a firm dissent based upon the mandates of conscience."[29] Here, King inextricably linked the prophetic tradition with what I've called participatory, principled patriotism. Yet that night he noted the warnings he'd received about the dangers of opposing an American war, divulging, "As I have called for radical departures from the destruction of Vietnam, many persons have questioned me about the wisdom of my path." Undoubtedly, King's stances late in life were perilous.

His assassination on April 4, 1968, is common knowledge, but less remembered is the inconvenient fact that at the time of his death MLK was highly unpopular. According to the Harris Poll in early 1968, King had a shocking 75 percent disapproval rating among

Americans. In fact, even in the early 1980s there was significant political pushback—mainly from Republicans—against the bill to designate Martin Luther King Jr. Day as a federal holiday. Ninety representatives and twenty-two senators voted against the bill in 1983, and as of 2015, eight (all Republicans) were still serving in Congress.[30] The now deceased, though all but canonized, seemingly moderate Senator John McCain was among their shameful number.

President Reagan, too, was a skeptic of the legislation and only signed it when it reached his desk with a veto-proof majority from Congress. Indeed, the very year he eventually approved the bill, Reagan had written that King's proposed holiday was "'based on an image, not reality," and he later said that "we will know in about 35 years" whether Dr. King had communist sympathies.[31] Clearly, King's racial, materialist, and antiwar dissent made lifelong enemies and generated lasting negative reverberations. Dissent often does. The prophetic strand of dissent didn't die with Martin Luther King Jr. Rather, it remains a potent force in contemporary America's nascent but still fervent antiwar movement. This is precisely why a sizable chunk of my public speeches are held in and sponsored by churches, often Unitarian but including a range of other Christian denominations.

The second tradition of dissent is the republican strand. This philosophy draws on the supposedly democratic and anti-imperial motivations of the rebelling colonists—known, fittingly, as "patriots"—in the American Revolution. The republican dissenters are far more secular and legalistic than the prophetics. They tend to see the nation's founding documents—notably the Declaration of

Independence and the US Constitution—as the core framework and source of American values.

Some, particularly doctrinaire libertarians, take this legalism a bit far and contend (in judicial circles the term is "originalism") that all contemporary judgments of public policy should be backward-looking and based on the original intent of the Founding Fathers. This, however, is decidedly problematic, seeing as the founders rarely agreed on much of anything at all, were—nearly to a man (and they were *all* men)—wealthy, and were often slaveholders too. The Constitution was nothing if not a compromise between contending special interests, regional concerns, and governmental ideologies. Nonetheless, as a starting institutional framework and emerging (evolving through the amendments process) guarantor of political rights and civil liberties, the Constitution remains a solid, if flawed, touchstone for patriotic dissent.

This is especially so if one adheres, as I do, to the progressional model of constitutionalism, based on the notion that the interpretation of the nation's founding documents can adapt and change according to the times. That should not imply, of course, that the Constitution ought to be considered a totally relativist instrument. Certainly, the core notions of its aspirational republicanism and rights guarantees must form a solid foundation for any evolving interpretation. That said, without some room for interpretive evolution, there would be little place for women's, gay, racial, or indigenous rights, among other concerns. Furthermore, while the Constitution doesn't explicitly take an anti-imperialist position, its checks on executive power and grounding in generally republican principles may reasonably be seen as thoroughly oppositional to empire.

Admittedly, as previously noted, it is my fixed position and that of most modern historians that the United States was, from the first, a continental settler-colonial empire built upon the "necessity"—and damning reality—of native displacement and destruction. Lest we forget, the nation's very Declaration of Independence refers unapologetically to "savage Indians." Nevertheless, the Constitution, viewed as an adaptational document, can ground the dissenting patriot's rebuke of aggressive militarism and expansionist imperialism, and it often has across the centuries.

In 1803, in the early days of the republic, opponents of President Thomas Jefferson's decision to buy from the French a massive swath of territory west of the nation's borders—the famed Louisiana Purchase—argued that the Constitution didn't allow for such expansion, at least unilaterally by the executive. Then in the 1820s and 1830s, challengers of President Andrew Jackson's Indian Removal Act of 1830 and general anti-native policies, which uprooted most tribes east of the Mississippi and forced them onto reservations further west, also sought relief in the courts through constitutional challenges. In the Supreme Court decision *Worcester v. Georgia*, they emerged victorious, at least technically. However, in a shockingly unconstitutional act, Jackson, dubbed King Andrew I by his opponents, flouted the court and proceeded apace with Indian displacement. He is reputed to have said of the Chief Justice of the Supreme Court, "John Marshall has made his decision; now let him enforce it!"[32] It was a flagrant taunt and hardly one of America's finest hours. Nonetheless, the challenge and tactics of the courageous dissenting defenders of native rights were squarely within the republican tradition.

The third strand of American dissent is the nationalist. Sometimes dark in its application and often in tension with the first two traditions, dissent on nationalist grounds generally involves the prioritization of perceived US interests over anything else. In that sense it can be associated with international relations theories of Realpolitik or realism. Nationalist dissent rejects universal (prophetic) or global (international law and norms) values and demotes the importance, in some cases, of even republican strictures. At its worst, nationalist opposition to a given policy can be insular and ethnocentric, to the point of conflating Americanism with whiteness or Protestantism and thereby justifying chauvinistic positions. As such, this form of dissent often flares up during periods of large-scale immigration and manifests in the long, cyclical tradition of American nativism.

While only infrequently staking unpopular or minority positions, nationalist dissenters have, at key points in American history, opposed foreign wars and empire expansion. More specifically, such dissidents have sometimes been—at least according to my own anti-imperial bias—right on foreign policy issues, even if often for the wrong reasons. For example, at the close of America's first "regime change" war (1846–48), some congressional opponents of the seriously considered plans for the annexation of Mexico in its entirety staked out a vaguely nationalist (though highly racist) challenge. For example, Senator John C. Calhoun of South Carolina, best known as a passionate defender of southern secessionism, argued against this "All Mexico" plan on the Senate floor on January 4, 1848, on the following grounds:

> We have never dreamt of incorporating into our Union any but the Caucasian race—the free white

> race. To incorporate Mexico, would be the very first instance of the kind, of incorporating an Indian race; for more than half of the Mexicans are Indians, and the other is composed chiefly of mixed tribes. I protest against such a union as that! Ours, sir, is the Government of a white race.[33]

While Calhoun and his colleagues staked out an important anti-annexationist, partly anti-conquest position in the midst of an aggressive war, the racism and white Protestant (most Mexicans were Catholic) chauvinism of their arguments were undoubtedly deplorable, if not atypical.

Half a century later, when the United States first meaningfully expanded outside North America's shores in the cessions gained after the Spanish-American War (1898), opponents of this European-style classic imperialism also sometimes peddled nationalist-flavored dissent. Usually what members of the Democratic Party—which was, then, the political entity most associated with the former Confederacy and the postwar South—most feared was that, just as had happened with most of the Western continental territories, new acquisitions such as the Philippines, Puerto Rico, and Guam would eventually be incorporated into the union as states. The problem from their perspective was that, far more than the lands wrested from Indians and Mexicans, these islands were both distant and densely populated with brown, "lesser," races.

That, it must be said, was the dark secret of turn-of-the-century "classic" anti-imperialism: a not insignificant segment of its adherents were unredeemable white supremacists. To complicate matters further, it is essential to recognize that quite often dissenters employ multiple strands of the tradition or straddle the lines between them. William Jennings Bryan, who certainly adhered to the prophetic practice, also traded in racialized, nationalistic, anti-imperial rhetoric. In 1900, during the bloody Philippine "Insurrection"—really a Filipino war of independence—Bryan declared:

> Some argue that American rule in the Philippine Islands will result in the better education of the Filipinos. Be not deceived . . . we dare not educate them, lest they learn to read the Declaration of Independence and Constitution of the United States and mock us for our inconsistency . . . The laboring man will be the first to suffer if oriental subjects seek work in the United States.[34]

Though less overt in his racism than Calhoun in the earlier era, Bryan clearly saw the incorporation of Catholic, brown Filipinos as citizens or laborers in the workforce as a definite threat.

To be fair, nationalist dissent is not always racist or nativist in character, though opponents of certain antiwar or anti-interventionist activists have, as we'll see, repeatedly tried to paint them with those very brushes. For example, the anti-interventionist movement of the interwar years (1919–41), traditionally pilloried as "isolationist," opposed America's involvement in another European war, partly through virulently nationalist positions. They argued—not altogether irrationally, given the unnecessary late-stage American bloodletting in the First World War[35]—that

US national interests wouldn't be served by entrance into another distant war across the seas.

They turned out to be mistaken regarding the level of definitively global threat that fascism (specifically German Nazism) posed, and as a result, traditional history has been rewritten to disparage their decidedly nationalist "America First" motto—Trump didn't invent the phrase—as inherently anti-Semitic. No doubt there were, in some isolationist circles, anti-Semites in the movement, but broad-brushing the entire anti-interventionist camp is inherently problematic. Such an expansive assertion implies that the US eventually entered the war on behalf of, or to halt the genocide of, Europe's Jews. Nothing could be further from the truth. President Roosevelt was well aware of the escalating atrocities in Hitler's Germany and even during the war did little to intervene (though his options were, admittedly, limited). America entered World War II because Japan attacked Pearl Harbor—the immediate catalyst for intervention—and, more acutely, because of the perceived geopolitical threat of a victorious, expansive Germany.

Even today, the charges of nativism, racism, and anti-Semitism against antiwar and anti-imperial activists haven't fully dissipated. Establishment interventionists and militarists—who, it must be said, constitute the majority of American political leaders since the Second World War—still use these pejorative labels as cudgels to bash foreign policy dissenters. Through such attacks the pro-war crowd seeks—and at this it often succeeds—to associate all antiwar dissenters with the dark side of the nationalist tradition, ignoring the fact that this is but one of the strands of opposition and the least prominent.

Consider the case of Andrew Bacevich. A West Point graduate, a Vietnam veteran, a retired US Army colonel, and subsequently a history professor and author of numerous books who lost a son to a bomb attack in the Iraq War, Bacevich emerged soon after 9/11 as a prominent critic of the "war on terror."[36] Throughout his postmilitary antiwar career, critics have (inaccurately) slandered him as an "isolationist." And, illustratively, in a January 2020 interview in the *New Yorker*, Bacevich, by then a recent cofounder of a new think tank (the Quincy Institute for Responsible Statecraft), was forced to field loaded, almost accusatory questions regarding what sitting Senator Tom Cotton (R-AR) called the Quincy Institute's "anti-Semitism."

Even a cursory read of the otherwise insightful interview demonstrates that the questioner sought to trap Bacevich in a racist or anti-Jewish retort or posture. The *New Yorker*'s Isaac Chotiner, champing at the bit throughout the exchange, posited the following statement (not exactly a question):

> The President who has been rhetorically the most anti-interventionist of any Republican or Democratic President, certainly in decades, is Donald Trump. Both Trump and [Fox News host Tucker] Carlson are the most racist people we've seen in their positions in a very long time. I don't think that's entirely a coincidence. Again, I'm not trying to say that means anti-interventionism is inherently racist, but I was curious whether you'd wrestled with that, and how it plays into your thinking.[37]

Characteristically, Bacevich was careful, measured, and kept his cool. His responses to the line of questioning and discussion on his previous statements regarding isolationism and to the charges that they were tinged with anti-Semitism, which made up fully one-third of the interview, were eloquent and effective. Bacevich, admitting that there are, perhaps, some racists in the Trump-supporting anti-interventionist wing of that coalition, stated:

> [If] I happen to be a white guy, but [with] a white male who is resentful with regard to the way the world is turning and who was looking for someone or something to blame, I can see the logical connection of that person saying that these efforts to somehow save the world, all those people out there who are not like me, which costs a lot of money, which costs American lives, all that's wrongheaded, I can see the logic of that. I just would resist the notion that therefore anybody who is an anti-interventionist somehow is a racist. I would reject that entirely.[38]

The inherent logic of Bacevich's response aside, what's most notable and demonstrative is that the conversation had to unfold at all. If a man with the honorifics and credentials of Bacevich—military academy grad, combat veteran, PhD, author, professor, Gold Star father—isn't exempt from specious charges of anti-Semitism, simply for being publicly anti-interventionist and anti- certain wars, then what hope does a more run-of-the-mill dissenting activist have to avoid trumped-up charges of nationalist-strand racism, nativism, and/or anti-Semitism? Precious little, I'd surmise.

THIS TAKES US TO THE FOURTH AND FINAL TRADITION OF dissent: the cosmopolitan. In direct opposition to the nationalist strand, this version of principled dissidence recognizes and celebrates the multi-ethnic and interfaith nature of the American body politic and, weaving together the prophetic and republican traditions, posits the need for internationally acceptable values and conduct. Seen in a certain light, cosmopolitan dissent is really a hybrid conglomeration of all the strands besides, for the most part, the nationalist. Perhaps Abraham Lincoln best personifies an early example of cosmopolitan dissent. He defended his anti–Mexican War, (eventually) antislavery, and (ultimately) antisecession stances with a combination of prophetic (universal religious values), republican (constitutional, "A house divided against itself cannot stand"), and cosmopolitan (waging aggressive war with Mexico would sully America's international reputation) rhetorical arguments. Lincoln might also have added that most of the Western world had abolished slavery by 1861.

Today, cosmopolitan dissenters—I count myself among them—judge the advisability, legality, and morality of American wars and general foreign policy on the basis of international law and norms; universal conceptions of human rights and dignity; republican, constitutional principles; diversity (social justice); *and* perceptions of national interests. In a certain sense, far from being the vaguely bigoted nationalist dissenter that the *New Yorker* seemed to imply he was, Andrew Bacevich is a quintessential cosmopolitan. A self-described Catholic conservative, he grounds his dissent in equal parts personal religious faith, principled republicanism, sober assessment of national interests, and respect for international values. The same could be said of Martin Luther King Jr. That's not bad company to keep.

This clearly most complex and multifaceted tradition of dissent developed over time and truly gained traction in the aftermath of the catastrophic, norms-shattering Second World War. Indeed, the often mocked, admittedly sometimes insincere but usually quite genuinely held self-identification as a "citizen of the world" is, for the most part, a product of postwar technological advances in travel and communication, disgust with nationalism-as-militarism, and the resultantly crafted international treaties and compacts. That said, participatory principled patriotism—and even the seeds of cosmopolitan informed dissent—has a long tradition in the United States (and elsewhere), one that has progressed over time and in response to both domestic and foreign events. My modern redefinition of dissent-as-patriotism, with its inherent cosmopolitan bent, is likely nebulous without some knowledge of this historical evolution.

4.

One of my favorite professors in graduate school at the University of Kansas was a peculiar Brit named J. C. D. Clark. His expertise was in early modern British political and social history, but he dabbled in lots of topics and could always be counted on for unique and erudite insights on a range of matters. I'll always remember his reflection on the almost never mentioned religious aspect of the American Revolution. He liked to say that because most modern historians are secular progressives, they tend to give short shrift to the deep-seated religious motivations of many prominent figures from the past. For example, *of course* religion played a role in inspiring colonial rebellion, when, after all, the American colonies and eventual republic were *founded* by Protestant dissenters—separatist opponents of the Church of England. He reminded us that whereas some 10 percent of Britons in the home islands were dissenters, something more to the tune of 90 percent of the American colonists were such.

Fitting, then, that despite its rarity, risks, and regular failures, a nation chock-full of dissenters from the start would still boast a proud tradition of patriotic opposition. What's more, many of the characters in this morality tale are quite famous, and their inclusion might even surprise many Americans. Most, of course, were relative unknowns, common folks, or, oftentimes, figures once prominent but now lost to history. Consider just a brief recounting of some of the more notable political and military dissenters opposed to the nation's usually unnecessary and unethical imperial wars.

FEW LAYPERSONS TODAY CAN ARTICULATE JUST WHAT THE WAR of 1812, America's first major war of choice as a republic, was fought for. What those few *do* tend to remember are patriotic anecdotes from a long-ago war: Andrew Jackson mowing down foolish redcoats at the Battle of New Orleans, Dolly Madison saving the portrait of George Washington just before the British burned down the capital, Francis Scott Key penning "The Star-Spangled Banner" as he observed the bombardment of Fort McHenry.[39] Yet the justifications for the United States' decision to declare the war were feeble and rather dubious. That might explain why its congressional vote is still the closest of any of America's officially sanctioned wars. Indeed, on many levels the War of 1812 was the most peculiar conflict in US history.

Sure, the British, then engaged in worldwide warfare with Napoleonic France, had seized American ships and impressed American sailors into the King's Navy. Then again, France had seized ships too. Furthermore, before the declaration of war, Great Britain had agreed to cease the practice. But the strange war was declared regardless and raged on for over two years. And, contrary to popular mythology, this was a war the US nearly lost, in which it invaded and attempted to conquer Canada, saw many slaves flee to the *British* side, and destroyed Native American power east of the Mississippi River. Nonetheless, what the war most persistently fashioned was a unique kind of chauvinistic American patriotism—a war fever that, then as now, especially pervaded the nation's South and West. In fact, the term *war hawk* was coined at the time to describe a zealous political proponent of fighting the British. The term *hawk* is with us still. And in case there was any doubt about the inherently militaristic nature of the United States, the new republic's very national anthem, which is patently a *war song*, was penned during observance of the war's battles.

Worse still, the war solved nothing. The Treaty of Ghent, which ended the war, changed *nothing.* There was no change of borders, and the British said nothing about impressment—the purported *casus belli.* So just what had those thousands died for?

Certainly no American victory had forced the British to the peace table. By 1814 the war had become a debacle. Two consecutive American invasions of Canada had been stymied. Napoleon was defeated in April 1814, and the British finally began sending thousands of regular troops across the Atlantic to teach the impetuous Americans a lesson—even burning Washington, DC, to the ground. (In fairness, it should be noted that the Americans had earlier done the same to the Canadian capital at York.) The US coastline was blockaded from Long Island to the Gulf of Mexico; despite a few early single-ship victories in 1812, by 1814 the US Navy was all but finished, the US Treasury was broke and defaulted (for the first time in the nation's history) on its loans and debt, and 12 percent of US troops had deserted during the war.[40]

The conflict did, however, breed perhaps the first generation of anti-(foreign-)war dissenters. These folks, mostly centered in merchant New England, had both pecuniary and principled reasons to oppose what was frankly an American war of choice with Great

Britain. Certainly, since the British Empire constituted their top trading partner, a war with the former Mother Country—and its powerful navy, in particular—would be bad for business. However, most of these dissidents held firmly to principle: specifically, the deep-seated, reflexive fears of most founders that overseas wars—and the raising of the large armies they require—would subvert the republic at home and potentially lead it down the road to American Empire. In fact, by war's end an entire major political party, the Federalists, so opposed the war that many members met in a convention to discuss how to not only end the conflagration but also potentially amend the Constitution—to reduce the Southern preponderance in Congress and raise the bar for war declarations—in order to ensure such a mistake would not be made again.

Even a few Democratic-Republicans, from the party of President James Madison, boarded the antiwar train. John Randolph expressed his amazement that his war hawk colleagues wished to "go to war without money, without men, without a navy! . . . The people will not believe it." He even added that it was America that was the aggressor, and he said of the invasion of Canada that "in the eye of heaven, we must appear like so many descendants of Cain, seeking to imbrue our hands in our brothers' blood!" Randolph's principled opposition cost him as badly as it would the more commonly antiwar Federalist Party. He lost his reelection campaign in 1813 and was labeled by his party mates as pro-British, a defeatist, and a spy.[41] Note that these are the same sort of attacks leveled at opponents of the post-9/11 "war on terror."

In later decades there was significant dissent within the *military* from first the Indian Removal policy and then the army's brutal, protracted Seminole War. Davy Crockett—both hero soldier and politician—turned on his former commander and party loyalist Andrew Jackson and voted against the 1830 Indian Removal Bill. It cost him his seat in the House and helped motivate his eventual (ultimately fatal) decision to migrate to Texas and join the garrison of Anglo rebels in the Alamo. He described his decision on the bill thus: "I voted against [the] Indian Bill, and my conscience yet tells me that I gave a good and honest vote, and one that I believe will not make me ashamed in the day of judgment."

Even more astonishingly, Brigadier General John Wool, the commander of the mission to force-march the Cherokee Tribe to Oklahoma during 1836–37 in the infamous Trail of Tears, which killed thousands of men, women, and children in the process, was himself to prove an unlikely dissenter. In this he risked all: his career and even his own freedom. He wrote complaints to the secretary of war, upbraided subordinates who abused Cherokees, and—against orders—made extra blankets and rations available to the tribe and even prosecuted Georgia and Alabama civilians who attacked Indians. Finally, he asked to be recalled. These actions landed him before a court of inquiry, where he was ultimately acquitted by his successor and future Mexican-American War hero General Winfield Scott. Unapologetic to the last, Wool claimed: "If I had acted otherwise than I did, I should have considered myself recreant to the sacred trust reposed in me."[42]

Taking a step further, as Wool addressed the court, he indicted the entire federal policy towards the Native American tribes when he stated:

> The course of justice and humanity are but the dictates of an enlarged and liberal policy. By such a course the Indians were taught that some remains of justice, some touches of feeling yet existed in the bosoms of white men.... Suppose a different course had been pursued—that every...oppression and cruelty was practiced towards them, and they could find no redress. Might they not justly say: We can but die, let us first be revenged?

This was a profound statement for a serving army general to publicly utter. His words obviously had some effect on Scott, for although neither general succeeded in saving the Cherokees or alleviating the suffering on the Trail of Tears, Wool's successor, too, dissented against government Indian policy. For in what must count as a far finer hour than his later famed amphibious invasion and conquest of Mexico, Scott, too, defied orders and—so startled was he by the high number of deaths—agreed to allow the next batch of Cherokees to postpone emigration until the weather improved and to go without forced military escort. Years later, Scott would even reveal his lifelong regret for his own role in Cherokee Removal.

Less than a decade after what was left of the Cherokee people had been relocated to Oklahoma, another episode, in which the same General Scott would play a prominent role, further revealed the rather old history of American political and military dissent. The Mexican-American War produced perhaps the nation's first mass antiwar movement. This was a war that President James Polk, an ardent expansionist, drummed up, lied about, and then deceitfully sold to Congress and the American people. Slowly and then more rapidly, a wide variety of public figures finally opposed this venal war of aggression. They included artists, famous politicians, and future Civil War generals.

One of the most famous military skeptics, at least in the next war, was Lieutenant Ulysses Grant, future general and president. Uncomfortable with the justifications for the Mexican War from the start, Grant, during the later lengthy occupation of Mexico City, wrote his wife that "Mexico is a very pleasant place to live because it is never hot nor ever cold, but I believe everyone is hartily [*sic*] tired of war . . . . I pity poor Mexico." Grant never forgot the horror of his first war and never forgave his country for its aggressive invasion. In 1879, a few years after leaving the White House, he told a journalist, "I do not think there was ever a more wicked war than that waged by the United States on Mexico. I thought so at the time, when I was a youngster . . . [The war] was one of the most unjust ever waged by a stronger against a weaker nation." In his memoirs, Grant went further and described the Civil War as "our punishment" for that "transgression." How right he was.

The Whigs, most of whom had followed their party leadership in feckless acquiescence to a war few had any enthusiasm for, were later transformed by the Mexican conflict. By war's end it was their finest hour but also perhaps their party's downfall. No one with even scant knowledge of American history would conclude that antiwar activism tends towards political success. Nevertheless, if most Whigs—afraid of suffering the extinction of the anti–War of

1812 Federalists—folded, a few in Congress, known as the "14 irreconcilables," showed courage from the start.

They were led by the indefatigable Rep. John Quincy Adams. When most Whigs gave in to Polk's reasoning for war, the seventy-eight-year-old Adams would have *none* of it. Not only was he totally opposed to "this most outrageous war," but he told a fellow Massachusetts congressman that he "hoped the officers would all resign & the men all desert!" One of his fellow "irreconcilables," Congressman Luther Severance of Maine, declared from the start—contradicting Polk's initial war justification—that "it is on *Mexican* soil that blood has been shed" and even averred that for their "manly resistance" the Mexicans should be "honored and applauded."

But it wasn't until the Whigs' stalwart party leader, Henry Clay, took a strong antiwar stand that most members changed course. The three-time failed presidential candidate was likely moved to a more vocal position of dissent after the death of his favorite son, Colonel Henry Clay Jr., at the Battle of Buena Vista. Struck with a bullet in the thigh, the younger Clay had then heroically protected his retreating soldiers before succumbing to a deluge of Mexican bayonets. He was just thirty-five. The elder Clay was somewhat comforted by the knowledge that his son, "if he were to die . . . preferred to meet death on the battlefield." However, Clay, never enthusiastic about the invasion—and having likely torpedoed his last presidential command due to his then muted critique—admitted to a friend, "That consolation would be greater, if I did not believe the Mexican War was unnecessary and of an aggressive character."

Matters began to shift by the summer of 1847, when journalists outside of New England had finally seen enough atrocities in Mexico to begin to condemn the war. The public intellectuals spoke out next. Henry David Thoreau spent a night in jail after he symbolically refused to pay his poll tax in protest of the war. He then delivered a famous lecture, "Civil Disobedience," which called for resistance against the government's immoral war effort. Other writers and poets, such as Ralph Waldo Emerson and James Russell Lowell, followed suit. Walt Whitman, initially a war supporter, published an editorial titled "American Workingmen, Versus Slavery," in support of the upstart Pennsylvania Democrat David Wilmot's ultimately failed "Proviso" stipulating that all forms of human bondage be prohibited in any land taken from Mexico. Whitman's dissent, certainly a slap in the face to his paper's conservative Democratic readership, got him fired from the *Brooklyn Daily Eagle*, where he'd served as an editor.

Still, the major turning point was clearly Henry Clay's profound decision, on November 13, 1847, to give a widely promoted speech—the finest of his long career—in his hometown of Lexington, Kentucky. After much soul-searching, realizing his presidential prospects were likely behind him, he decided to boldly and publicly oppose the war that had cost him his son. A newly elected young freshman congressman from Illinois, Abraham Lincoln, was in attendance, having fortuitously stopped in the town to visit his wife's family en route to Washington, DC. What Clay said shocked his party and the nation.

He asserted that the US should never have annexed Texas in the first place, and then he proceeded not only to attack the obvious target, President Polk, but also to excoriate the vast majority of his *own* party, who had expediently voted for the war in 1846. The war had resulted in a "mad sacrifice of human life . . . waste of human treasure . . . mangled bodies . . . death and desolation." It was Mexico, not the US, that was "defending her firesides, her castles, her altars." The consequences, he said, were substantial. America had ceded its "unsullied" international "character." The only moral course, Clay declared, was for Congress to use its constitutional powers to cut off funds, end the war, and refuse to annex even a square mile of Mexican land. Now and in the future, America should disavow "any desire . . . to acquire any foreign territory . . . for the purpose of introducing slavery into it." In a radical step for a Kentuckian, Clay added, whether true or not, that he had "ever regarded slavery as a great evil."

Clay's hopes for the presidency may well have been gone. His melancholy over his son's death may have contributed. Nonetheless, the renowned orator's two-and-a-half-hour speech was incredibly courageous and, more importantly, widely influential. Thanks to the wonders of technology (which his Whig party had long championed), specifically the telegraph, Clay's remarks boomeranged across the entire country within days. Democratic papers unsurprisingly labeled Clay a traitor. President Polk's favored newspaper, the *Washington Union*, condemned Clay's remarks as "the spirit of treason promulgated." No matter, this single speech catalyzed and exploded the nascent antiwar movement. That faction was no longer a New England phenomenon. At rallies across the nation, from Indiana to Kentucky to New Jersey to Maine, thousands denounced the war and read Clay's speech aloud.

The Lexington speech may also, most enduringly, have forever altered the career and even character of that young congressman in the audience, Abraham Lincoln. Before the Lexington talk, Lincoln was a "tariff man," a domestic policy wonk, with little interest in foreign affairs. He hadn't planned to kick off his freshman term in

Washington on an antiwar platform. Yet despite hailing from an enthusiastically pro-war Illinois district, that's just what he did. No doubt Lincoln foresaw the political consequences. Perhaps he thought that if Clay could demonstrate political bravery, then so should he.

So it was, then, that on December 22, 1847, Lincoln, the unknown (and sole Whig) congressman from Illinois proceeded to deliver a bold first speech on the House floor. As a well-trained country lawyer, Lincoln's inaugural remarks were more methodical than inspirational, but other members took notice as he effectively battered away at President Polk's initial (deceptive) justification for the invasion. American blood, Lincoln asserted, *had* been shed, but in a "contested region" by "armed officers and soldiers, sent into that settlement by the military orders of the President," and the loss thus could not be blamed on the defensive Mexican troopers. According to Lincoln, Polk, though seduced by "military glory," must in his heart be "deeply conscious of being in the wrong—that he feels the blood of this war, like the blood of Abel, is crying to Heaven against him."

Congressman Lincoln's speech and early votes didn't endear him to his pro-war constituents. Though his remarks brought him the *national* renown so rare for an obscure freshman representative, the blowback—particularly back in Illinois—was severe. One prominent Democratic paper labeled Lincoln a new Benedict Arnold. His own local *State Register* seconded the notion and declared: "Henceforth will the Benedict Arnold of our district be known here only as the Ranchero Spotty [slang for a Mexican guerrilla fighter] of *one term*." Lincoln's own law partner in Springfield warned him that his antiwar position constituted "political suicide." Unfazed, Honest Abe doubled down. On January 12, 1848, he again spoke—for 45 minutes—

and declared that President Polk should "remember he sits where Washington sat . . . As a nation should not, and the Almighty will not, be evaded, so let him attempt no evasion—no equivocation." It ought to come as no surprise that Abraham Lincoln was just a single-term congressman.

If Lincoln was the newest antiwar voice on Capitol Hill, though a virulent one, former President John Quincy Adams was most certainly the eldest and ablest. Indeed, opposition to the Mexican-American War would constitute his final mortal act. As the historian Richard Immerman adeptly stated, "Adams [had] never voted to withhold appropriations from the soldiers, but . . . on Feb. 21, 1848, he cast his final vote against a resolution to commend America's victorious generals." It is fitting that when the clerk called for a roll call on the routine measure, Adams bellowed his last word in Congress: "No!" He then slumped over at his desk. Eighty years old, he had suffered a massive stroke, and he soon lapsed into unconsciousness. Before he did, he gathered the strength to ask for Henry Clay, who grasped his hand and wept over him. Two days later, the only ex-president to leave the White House for a career in Congress was dead.

The young Lincoln—representative of the "new blood" in the revamped Whig Party—had witnessed Adams's dramatic collapse on the House floor. No doubt he was soon surprised to learn he'd been chosen to serve as one of the old man's pallbearers at the forthcoming elaborate state funeral. One wonders what effect these theatrical events had on the future president, how it influenced his career. We know that a few days later Lincoln cast his first antislavery vote as a congressman. Adams's death, coming on top of Clay's histrionic speech, also seemed to buoy the Whig Party. Though they never cut off funds or supplies to the troops, Whig congressmen never acted on Polk's two requests for reinforcements for the occupation of Mexico, and—in a prelude to modern political drama—they actually lowered the ceiling on federal borrowing.

Clay must have known his Lexington speech ruined any remaining hope he'd had for his party's 1848 nomination; it would go instead to the more electable and less controversial General Zachary Taylor. Furthermore, though Clay reentered the Senate in 1849 and worked hard to forge (unsuccessfully, it turned out) a compromise in 1850 to avert civil war, the antiwar and, by extension, anti-slave-state-expansion positions he'd staked out in his speech ultimately proved the undoing of the Whig Party within a decade. But that didn't make him or Lincoln *wrong*. Historically, the principled, patriotic dissenters rarely are.

EXACTLY FIFTY YEARS AFTER THE UNITED STATES GOVERNMENT stole the north half of Mexico over the howls emanating from America's first significant national antiwar movement, Uncle Sam took imperialism global for the first time. Suffice it to say, a new president, William McKinley, a Republican this time—empire is the one lasting bipartisan American enterprise—responded to a growing tide of expansionist rhetoric that called for the US to take its values and, more importantly, its economic goods and military defenders of such overseas. The European empires, then at their ravenous zenith, had already snatched up nearly every speck of the planet, and if Washington didn't get in on the game, they feared, America would lose both international prestige and market share. So McKinley—as an odd precursor to George W. Bush a century hence—found a suitable pretense and took the country to war with Spain. That crumbling and by then third-rate empire quickly collapsed, and the US went ahead and seized all of its Caribbean and Pacific possessions, most notably the highly populated Philippine Islands.

That said, the intellectual muses of this particular American pivot towards overt overseas maritime imperialism were bookish academic types and decidedly *not* situated in the traditional corridors of power. Nevertheless, as has occasionally happened in US history, their theories gained immense momentum and for a time catapulted them to national prominence. The first was a civilian academic, Frederick Jackson Turner, the other a US Navy captain, Alfred Thayer Mahan, with more passion for theorizing than seafaring. Both—the former indirectly, the latter gleefully—supplied the cerebral horsepower for war with Spain and the proceeding decades of imperial policing and suppression.

In 1890 the distinguished American historian Frederick Jackson Turner combed the latest US census and declared, in a widely read speech, that the American "frontier" was officially "closed." He meant, of course, that there were no longer any uncharted Western lands to explore or Indian tribes to fight. The West was conquered and "civilized," once and for all. According to Turner, westward expansion had defined American history and values. "Civilizing" the West, through hardy individualism and strife, had altered and established the American soul. In his telling, which was very influential in its day, the "loss" of the frontier wasn't necessarily a good thing; in fact, it had the potential to "soften" Americans and rot the foundation of the republic.

It was believed that without new lands to conquer, new space in which to expand, Americans would become a sedentary people riven with the same class divisions and social conflict infecting Europe. Furthermore, without new markets, how would American farmers and manufacturers maintain and improve their economic situation? The West was an idea, mostly, but it spoke to an inherently American trait: expansionism. Ours was a society of more: more land, more profits, more freedom, more growth. In a view widely held then as now, the US would die if it ever stopped expanding. "From sea to shining sea" wasn't enough; no two oceans should hem in American markets, the American people, or American ideals. This was and is the fervent nature of the American experiment, for better or worse.[43]

Alfred Thayer Mahan was the son of a West Point professor and served in the US Navy for almost forty years, including the Civil War. During the final third of his career, Mahan, always most comfortable in the classroom, taught at and then headed the newly established Navy War College. In 1890 Mahan published *The Influence of Sea Power upon History, 1660–1783*, which argued that naval supremacy had been for many centuries the prime determinant of national economic and geopolitical power. In 1897 in *The Interest of America in Sea Power, Present and Future*, he overtly encouraged his fellow Americans, particularly elite power brokers, to invest even more in maritime power and, more importantly, to accept their national responsibilities to shed their old continental cautions and journey deep into the blue water and seize and hold colonies, bases, and coaling stations.[44]

That's where Mahan, the navy booster, converged with Turner, the Western continental frontier guy. With the frontier "closed" and thus nowhere else to settle the growing population (actually there was and still is plenty of space in the expansive continental United

States) or, it was assumed, markets left to open for the goods they produced, the old "frontier line" would in the new century just have to be jumped tens of thousands of miles west into the Pacific Ocean and south down to the Caribbean and South America. The logic was faulty, the presumptions grandiose and chauvinistic. No matter, the DC crowd was mostly all in, and much of the population bought the rather simplistic logic hook, line, and sinker.

Not everyone, however, was "on board" with Mahan's (personally) ship-starved maritime-imperialist theories. Though the actual war with Spain wrapped up in just a few months and produced remarkably few American casualties, the subsequent occupation of the Philippines and the fifteen-year fight to suppress nationalists there would prove the true crucible of the era. *That* war, America's longest continual combat action until the ongoing Afghanistan War surpassed it in 2017, would cough up its fair share of hawkish blowhards and abhorrent war criminals, but it also, for a time, breathed life back into the nation's *second* mass antiwar and anti-imperialist movement.

Few Americans remember the US invasion, occupation, and pacification—a neat euphemism, that—of the Philippine Islands, but Filipinos will never forget. Perhaps half a million locals died, one-sixth of the total population, at the hands of superior US military technology, exacerbated health crises, and starvation. The war bloodied and frustrated the US Army, too. Some four thousand soldiers died (a casualty count comparable to that of the recent, ongoing Iraq War), many more were wounded, and the conventional conflict and counterinsurgency raged from 1898 to 1913, making the Philippine-American War the second longest in American history, after Afghanistan.

For all the villains in this story, there were (and always are) Americans willing to dissent against overseas conquest and imperialism. Indeed, they were a large, diverse lot and sometimes rather peculiar bedfellows. They were, too, the heroes of the era. From the very start of the Philippine occupation, many prominent citizens publicly opposed the war. Some among this coalition of intellectuals, politicians, artists, and businessmen may have acceded to the conquest of native and Mexican lands but saw imperial expansion overseas as un-American and unconstitutional. Throughout the era they made their voices heard and fought for the soul of the nation.

Skeptics across the spectrum of public life would form the Anti-Imperialist League, which, at its height, had hundreds of thousands of members, making it one of the largest antiwar organizations in American history and an impressive achievement in a period of such intense martial fervor. The leaders of the movement included Democratic Party stalwart (and noted prophetic-strand dissenter) William Jennings Bryan, the magnate Andrew Carnegie (who offered to buy the Philippines from the US government in order to set the islands free!), the social activist Jane Addams, the labor organizer Samuel Gompers, the civil rights leader Booker T. Washington, former President Grover Cleveland, former President Benjamin Harrison, and, of course, the ever-indefatigable Mark Twain. What the members of this diverse group had in common was a profound sense that imperialism was antithetical to the idea of America.

Bryan, one of the great orators of the day, summarized this notion when he proclaimed that "the imperialistic idea is directly antagonistic to the idea and ideals which have been cherished by the American people since the signing of the Declaration of Independence." The politician and Civil War veteran Carl Schurz compared the Filipino rebels favorably to the colonial patriots and asked what Americans would do if the natives refused to submit: "Let soldiers marching under the Stars and Stripes shoot them down? Shoot them down because they stand up for their independence?" Of course, that is precisely what countless members of the US military would proceed to do, under orders from their officers, generals, and ultimately the president.

The Anti-Imperialist League won many moral but few practical victories. Part of the reason for this was the US government's overt suppression of civil liberties. Famously, in what became known as the "mail war," the postmaster general ordered that anti-imperialist literature mailed to soldiers in the Philippines be confiscated. Artists and cultural critics then took the anti-imperial fight to the public. The most prominent and outspoken was Mark Twain, and this, more than his famous books, marked the man's finest hour. He announced his stand in late 1900, stating: "I have seen that we do not intend to free, but to subjugate the people of the Philippines. We have gone there to conquer, not to redeem . . . . And so I am an anti-imperialist." Some called it treason, others patriotism.

Eventually, and remarkably, genuine anti-imperialist sentiments even made it into the official platform of the Democrats, then as now one of the two mainstream political parties. Imagine a major party platform *today* declaring: "We oppose militarism. It means conquest abroad and intimidation and oppression at home. It means the strong arm which has been ever fatal to free institutions." Never happen, right? Well, the 1904 platform was (mostly) noble indeed, at least with regard to war and imperialism. But these sentiments and the party that espoused them ultimately lost—clearly not atypical in America's past.

Theodore Roosevelt, the national cheerleader of imperialism, easily retained the presidency in the election that year, having earlier risen from the vice presidency when McKinley was assassinated in 1901. Nevertheless, in the election there had been an exceedingly rare referendum on the nature of the national soul, but sadly, too many American voters (then all male and nearly all white) chose war, conquest, and annexation.[45] Still, even though Teddy had earlier declared the Philippine-American War officially "over" on—what a coincidental date—July 4, 1902, in reality serious combat continued for almost ten years after his successful 1904 election.

NOT LONG AFTER THE PHILIPPINE-AMERICAN WAR—significant combat actions continued until 1913—the great imperial powers of Europe went mad and were soon at war. Less than three years after that, in April 1917, America would enter the conflagration and contribute quite a bit of its own blood, though far less than its allies and adversaries. The very next year, in the midst of Uncle Sam's new war, its first ever fought on the European continent, a great but now mostly forgotten American dissident—in a war that produced many—declared: "War is the health of the state."

So said the eerily prescient and uncompromising antiwar radical Randolph Bourne in the very midst of what Europeans called the Great War, a nihilistic conflict that eventually consumed the lives of at least nine million soldiers, including some fifty thousand Americans. He meant, ultimately, that wars—especially foreign wars—inevitably increase the punitive and regulatory power of government. He opposed what Americans now call the First World War on these principled grounds. Though he'd soon die an early death, Bourne had correctly predicted the violations of civil liberties, deceptive propaganda, suppression of immigrants, vigilantism, and press restriction that would result on the home front as American boys were being slaughtered in the trenches of France.

This, the war on the free press, free speech, and dissent more generally, is the true legacy of the American war in Europe of 1917–18.

The primary tool of oppression for the US government was the Sedition Act, overwhelmingly passed into law on May 16, 1917. The impetus for the bill was Attorney General Thomas Gregory's request for an amendment to the press-constricting Espionage Act that would allow him to prosecute "disloyal utterances." The result was a new law that prohibited "any disloyal, profane, scurrilous, or abusive language about the form of government . . . or Constitution . . . or flag of the United States, or the uniform of the Army or Navy." Beyond the law's troubling and obvious attack on free expression, the very vagueness of the statute lent itself to abuse.

It was the fanatic Attorney General Gregory who would wield this new tool of federal oppression. The Texan performed his duties with glee, stating of war opponents: "May God have mercy on them, for they need expect none from an outraged people and an avenging government." It didn't take particularly violent or catalyzing speech to earn an arrest, conviction, and federal prison sentence. When a New Hampshire citizen cited his opinion that "this was a [banker J. P.] Morgan war and not a war of the people," he received a three-year prison sentence.

More famously, when the prominent Socialist leader Eugene V. Debs delivered an antiwar speech in Canton, Ohio, which focused mainly on the purported ills of capitalism and didn't explicitly urge violation of conscription laws, he was arrested and earned a ten-year bid in the federal penitentiary. Ultimately, the martyrdom of Debs partly backfired. Running for the presidency from federal prison in 1920, he earned nearly a million votes, the highest popular vote percentage by a Socialist in American history.

No court challenges of the deplorable Sedition Act bore fruit, and the law remained on the books until it was repealed in December 1920. By then the war was over, precedent was set, and the damage was done. Many languished in prison for years for the crimes of war opposition and criticism. As historian David M. Kennedy concluded, "Commentators ever since have rightly viewed it as a landmark of repression in American history . . . . It reveals a great deal about the popular temper at the midpoint of American belligerency."[46] Indeed it was and did.

That the Sedition Act needed to be used so broadly deflates the myth that Americans rushed en masse to recruiting stations and waged war with great enthusiasm. In reality, when the government called for one million military volunteers, only 73,000 enlisted. Six weeks later the US settled on conscription. In the course of the war, 330,000 Americans were officially classified as war evaders and thousands of pacifists were detained in conscientious objector military camps, where they were forced to prove the veracity of their claims.

One outgrowth of the government war on dissent—and the failed yet furious counteraction—was the formation of what later became the still prominent (if controversial) American Civil Liberties Union (ACLU). The battles waged by the new organization and countless more grassroots protests against the war and liberty violations demonstrated the potential power and vigorous persistence of dissenters. The battle rages again today, as after 9/11 to be antiwar, liberal, or even libertarian is to be brushed with the toxic brand of "Un-Americanism."[47] In this sense, if the proud pantheon of political and military dissenters during that war were, despite their sacrifices, ultimately vindicated by historical scholars, their ostracization and later trivialization set a troubling precedent.

There was, however, following the absurd bloodletting of World War I, a rare yet profound moment of popular American caution and skepticism regarding the advisability and morality of getting involved in future wars. It was a brief, passing phase, ultimately, beginning in 1919 and brought to an abrupt close with the outbreak of World War II and the necessity of defeating Adolf Hitler and the Nazi Germans. Yet, though largely erased from the present consciousness—breezed over in most American history courses between lessons on the "Roaring Twenties," the Great Depression, and the Second World War ("the Good War"[48])—the era remains important and instructive as a demonstration of what popular antiwar dissent *could* be.

One track of this dissent worth homing in on—though not at the expense of vital civilian action—is that which flowed and flows from *within* the ranks of soldiers and veterans. After all, today more than ever, the military is a widely respected institution—so much so, in fact, that many citizens lend extra credence and credibility to the views of veterans, especially combat veterans. And though their efforts did not always engender immediate or short-term success, the rare but historically pervasive breed of military antiwar dissenters has often made a public splash and had disproportionate influence on public debate. This has often been true despite the best efforts of pro-war, more powerful interests to silence them or erase them from popular memory after the fact. Their story—and in a sense my own—is worth recounting.

5.

A republic, however flawed from its inception it may be, is most likely to lose its way, to shred its institutions and betray its promise, through the execution of aggressive war, militarism, and imperial pretensions. That, after all, is how the Roman Republic died—a republic, it must be said, that the founding generation was quite literally obsessed with.

Read the nation's founding documents, read the personal papers and correspondence of its most famous inaugural generation, or just walk the avenues of Washington, DC, and gaze upon the Greco-Roman architecture of the public buildings and you'll see this couldn't be clearer. The founders were preoccupied with, even tormented by, the Roman Republic and the question of why it ultimately fell and transformed into an empire. This was the quandary of their generation, and it is fitting that the dissent upon which I focus herein is on anti-imperialism. Washington, Adams, Jefferson, perhaps even Hamilton would approve.

So in my assessment anti-imperialism is as American as apple pie. Unfortunately, that tradition is lost in the modern age, definitely since the mandatory faux patriotism reigned in the wake of the 9/11 attacks and, if we're honest, probably since the US government convinced itself and its people that America singlehandedly won the Second World War, never mind the twenty million Soviets who died in it. Ever seen one of those flippant, absurdly inaccurate but shockingly popular T-shirts that read: "USA: Back-to-Back World War Champs"? I have, and they make me sick. As a historian I know the truth: French blood and, to a lesser extent, British won the First World War—which we entered at the eleventh hour—and rivers of Russian blood won the Second World War. The US effort was relatively small potatoes in the first war but a disproportionate contributor in the second. Still, as the saying goes: "When the legend becomes fact, print the legend." America sure has.

Dissent, like most complex human endeavors, defies simple categorization. There are many reasons, rarely straightforward, that one might choose to oppose one's government or its policies. Prophetic religious values, republican principles, national interests, and universal humanist ethics usually combine, on one level or another, to inform the dissenter. Such is the intricacy and thus the beauty of the patriotic dissident.

Still, I'd be remiss if I didn't lament the state of dissent, of antiwar activism, of patriotic opposition in my own day. Consider the small university town of Lawrence, Kansas, where, for proximity to my children, I choose to make my life. Home to the University of Kansas (KU), replete with nearly thirty thousand students, the "People's Republic" of Lawrence is a liberal oasis in a sea of intolerant militarist red. It has a storied progressive history, founded as it was by transplanted idealist New England abolitionists intent on ensuring the newest American territory would be "free," meaning free of slavery. From 1854 to 1865 eastern Kansas was a battleground between free and slave interests engaged in a microcosmic civil war that presaged the nation's conflagration. It was here that the radical millenarian abolitionist warrior John Brown—who still has beers, T-shirts, and bars dedicated to him today in town—first made a name for himself. And, notably, first pro-slavery rebels and then a Confederate guerrilla army during the Civil War burned Lawrence to the ground, twice.

So imagine my dismay when, on January 25, 2020, an established anti–Iran War international "day of action," fewer than ten students showed up for the protest rally I keynoted. I asked, flippantly, early in my speech, whether anyone else had heard of the major research university four blocks to the west of our rally, and I wondered aloud if any of the students might consider shaking off their hangovers and looking up from their iPhones long enough to actually rally for a good cause in the company of other actual human beings. My remarks engendered a good laugh, which is always welcome, but I was serious, genuinely pained by the near absence of students at this protest regarding what I took to be *the* issue of the moment.

What a shameful fall from grace for a college and a city that were a veritable war zone in the aftermath of President Nixon's Cambodia invasion and the killing of four students at Kent State University. Hundreds protested, then thousands. The student union building was burned, gunfire exchanged with the police, the National Guard called in, and the entire city placed under curfew for a few days. Indeed, little Lawrence was for years a flashpoint city in the anti–Vietnam War movement.[49]

What, one might reasonably ask, is the variable—the major difference—between the KU students of 1970 and the KU students fifty years later? To me the answer is simple: the draft. During the

Vietnam War, even college students, who were deferred while enrolled in classes, faced the prospect of military service, potentially even combat, upon graduation. Nothing so motivates a young adult to follow foreign policy, to weigh the advisability or morality of an ongoing war, as the possibility of having to put "skin in the game." Without at least the potential requirement to serve in the military and in one of America's now countless wars, an entire generation—or really two, since Nixon ended the draft in 1973—has had the luxury of ignoring the ills of US foreign policy, to distance themselves from its reality.

It's about fairness and justice, sure, but it's also a question of the health of what remains of the republic. With the American people absenting themselves from the responsibilities or even potentialities of service, the *other 1 percent*—as I like to call today's military class—becomes a sort of Roman Praetorian Guard, rotated in and out of combat again and again like so many mercenaries. This isn't an attack on the courage or competence of a generation of soldiers, of whom more has been asked than perhaps any before, but rather a regretful diagnosis of a civil-military gap that unfairly sacrifices the freedom and physical safety of some for the convenience of the masses. Furthermore, this gap has stifled antiwar and anti-imperial dissent and seemingly will continue to do so.

That was Tricky Dick's whole point. Nixon may have been an uncouth, corrupt monster, but he was one hell of a crafty politician and always knew what he was doing. During the tail end of the Vietnam War, Nixon was veritably obsessed with the growing mass antiwar movement. Always a paranoid man who saw enemies around every corner, the classically insecure president never handled criticism well. By the early 1970s, with the failing war still a morass, Nixon all but declared war on what he labeled “un-American,” “communist-inspired” antiwar activists, especially student ones. He sought to destroy them, indirectly, and deflate the motivation and energy that fueled the movement.[50] How better to accomplish this than to eliminate conscription, to transition to an “all-volunteer” force (AVF)?

The ever-cynical Nixon grasped one profound, if inconvenient, truth about many young peace activists: they were as much, if not more, anti*draft* as they were anti*war*. Selfishness, Nixon knew as well as anyone, is, for better or worse, a core aspect of the human condition. So he largely succeeded in taking much of the steam out of the protests by decreasing troop levels in Vietnam, concurrently escalating aerial bombardment of enemy cities, conducting illegal bombings of neighboring Laos and Cambodia in secret, and—most vitally—taking most (particularly privileged) Americans’ “skin” out of “the game.”[51] Draft calls rapidly decreased and then ended completely and US troop deaths plummeted (but certainly not Vietnamese casualties), until Nixon “succeeded,” by 1973, in negotiating “peace with honor” and, he hoped, in managing a (face-saving) “decent interval,” as he called it, between the peace accords and the eventual conquest of South Vietnam by the Communist North.

That’s just it. Nixon never really believed the US could “win” in Vietnam. That war wasn’t even a top priority for him; rather, it was an inherited nuisance, and, like the presidents who preceded him, he simply didn’t want to be remembered as the one who “lost” Vietnam. His ire towards those protesting nemeses of his was all about *power*, specifically his instinctual aversion to anyone—politician or protestor—having the temerity to question his power. Nixon never got his decent interval, of course. He was forced to resign from office in 1974 after his insane levels of corruption—mainly surrounding his cover-up of the break-in to the Democratic National Committee headquarters in the Watergate building by some of his minions—and left his successor, Vice President Gerald Ford, holding the proverbial bag when, just over two years after the Paris Peace Accords, the North Vietnamese Army swallowed South Vietnam whole.

Would that the tragic story had ended there. Only Nixon, probably to a degree even he couldn't have imagined, had far more lasting and detrimental repercussions for civil-military relations, republican discourse, and the very traditions of American dissent. The reverberations and costly second- and third-order effects remain. Military service has become "optional," the responsibility of a tiny professional warrior caste. Though this all-volunteer force proved remarkably disciplined and tactically competent, it has been strategically ineffective. With the exception of limited, lopsided conflicts—Grenada (1983), Panama (1989), Desert Storm (1990–91)—it has failed to win a single major war. It muddled through to failure in its intervention into the Lebanese Civil War (1982–84), and since 9/11 it has foundered—and remains ensconced—in Afghanistan, Iraq, and Syria. Furthermore, the AVF's expansive efforts to train, supply, advise, and assist indigenous security forces in dozens of nations from West Africa to Central Asia have often proved counterproductive (generating more terror outfits) and bloodier than expected.[52]

Besides efficacy, there are serious questions regarding the AVF's fairness and just how "voluntary" the all-volunteer force is. Beyond relieving the vast majority of the populace of any responsibility to serve, sacrifice, or even *follow* American foreign and war-making policy, the lack of a draft has added major stressors to the careers of those who do fight. A generation of professional warriors that has repeatedly deployed faces a mental health crisis of the first order, littered with substance-abuse problems, in addition to the obvious loss of seven thousand dead soldiers and upwards of fifty-two thousand physically wounded.[53] What's more, the strain of repetitive and geographically expansive deployments has stretched the capabilities of the active-duty force to its limits. As a result, the National Guard and reserve components—designed to be a *strategic* reserve in the event of a major war—have been regularly thrown into the fray, thereby transformed into a go-to operational ready reserve.[54]

Nor does the US military any longer *look* like America. The AVF, as it nears its fiftieth anniversary, is highly unrepresentative of the populace writ large. Today, the average American trooper is slightly poorer, more rural, Southern, and likely to have a family legacy in the military life. Elites have opted out fully. No longer do the scions of Ivy League families serve the nation—over four hundred Harvard graduates died in World War II, whereas in the fall semester of 2014, Harvard, Yale, and Princeton *combined* counted only eight undergraduate veterans *enrolled*—let alone athletes, celebrities, or the progeny of politicians. As prominent critics of the unfairness and ineffectiveness of the AVF, retired Army Major General Dennis Laich and retired Colonel Lawrence Wilkerson summarized:

> Further, that 1 percent [that serves] does not come primarily or even secondarily from the families of the Ivy Leagues, of Wall Street, of corporate leader-

> ship, from the Congress, or from affluent America; it comes from less well-to-do areas: West Virginia, Maine, Pennsylvania, Oklahoma, Arkansas, Mississippi, Alabama, and elsewhere. For example, the Army now gets more soldiers from the state of Alabama, population 4.8 million, than it gets from New York, Chicago, and Los Angeles combined, aggregate metropolitan population more than 25 million. Similarly, 40 percent of the Army comes from seven states of the Old South.[55]

Among the many dangers of such an unequal state of affairs is that, naturally, as overburdened, unreflective, yet hyperadulated military professionals—mainly inhabiting bases far from major cities and situated in the Deep South, Midwest, and Great Plains—sense their divergence from civil society, their profound "otherness," they'll succumb to the cardinal sin of the soldier: self-righteousness.

I've felt the tug of sanctimoniousness myself in the past, seen the trait rear its ugly head among peers and superiors alike, watched in dismay as today's politicians of both major parties increasingly bow to the supposed superiority of senior military leaders. While an outright military coup may still (one hopes) be a long shot in this country, consider the recent, almost unprecedented infusion of generals into one presidential administration after another. In a handful of cases, even active-duty flag officers have served in core, patently political positions within the executive national security establishment. Absent any particular critique of the competence and character of these career professionals, the recent proliferation of generals in the White House ought to be disturbing in a country that ostensibly prides itself on its tradition of civilian control of the military. Matters have soared pretty far off the rails of civilian-led republicanism in the curious (but still instructive) case of Donald Trump, when the media deemed the three generals on his senior staff to be democracy's last, best hope and dubbed them the "*adults* in the room."[56]

All of this—Nixon's gambit, the evolution of the AVF, and the saturation of generals in unelected but vital governmental positions—has had and will continue to have distressing implications for the proud tradition of patriotic American dissent. Absent conscription, an uninvolved public majority has opted out of military service or even the imagination of military service, collectively chosen a combination of apathy and anemic soldier adulation, and opted for the luxury of mostly ignoring foreign affairs or the nation's endless wars. This hasn't boded well for the development of any sort of mass citizens' antiwar movement, certainly nothing on the scale of the Vietnam-era protests of my parents' generation. The salient question is, what is the missing (or added) variable today? As an unashamed Luddite, I'd love to blame it all on the mindless distraction of self-absorbed technological culture. But, truthfully, there's something else afoot.

The absent contemporary variable is the draft. If the mothers of teenage sons had to worry about little Johnny's potential conscription and if twenty-two-year-old college students nearing graduation had to stare down the prospect of draft eligibility, then I for one would bet on a whole lot more international sections of newspapers being read and plenty of extra students showing up at the local antiwar rallies. Sad, isn't it, that one potential solution to *less* war might just be *more* military service. Nor is this something to be argued lightly; serious issues of loss of bodily and emotional autonomy are associated with mandatory conscription. Then again, desperate times—and America's no-end-in-sight, longest-ever wars certainly qualify—often call for desperate measures. The United States, maybe more than ever before, desperately needs a massive, public, empowered antiwar and anti-imperial dissenting wave to crash on its shores and across its vast interior. The survival of the republic—at least of what it aspires to be—may well depend on it.

Where, then, in a time where my suggestions about the value of reinstating the draft are purely hypothetical because there is absolutely no political appetite for conscription, does that leave the antiwar movement, the patriotic dissenters? Just a bit hopeless and fatalistic, on the one hand, but on the other, all is not lost. The moment may have arrived at which, with no disrespect to the many diehard civilian activists, combat veterans must step up and form a vanguard of sorts for revitalized patriotic dissent. The reason is as simple as it is, in a way, disquieting: Americans inherently trust their veterans and imbue them with credibility. Though it is deeply unsettling when the citizens of a republic *only* believe in one public institution, the military, the contemporary crisis is such that socially conscious veterans of these endless, fruitless wars must use that (perhaps undeserved) credibility and turn it against the militarist elites who have taken Washington hostage.

Make no mistake: this is nothing less than a call to arms. But in *this* war, our weapons will be our pens, laptops, and booming voices. It may just be the most valuable service a generation of dismayed veterans will have ever rendered to the nation and Constitution they love and swore to protect.

It is undoubtedly a long shot, a veritable Hail Mary of catalyzed dissent. Still, nothing is totally hopeless, nothing is inevitable, and always contingent is the course of human events. Today's antiwar, anti-imperial dissenting veteran patriots can draw solace from a proud pantheon of combat-proven opponents of ill-advised or immoral American conflagrations. It is, one assumes purposefully, a history rarely, if ever, taught in this country's public schools. Unless one studies American history at the graduate level in a major research or liberal arts university, one is highly unlikely to come across the long tradition of veteran dissenters.

Nonetheless, try as the powerful may, no one can wholly erase that crucial past. Ever since the American Revolution, the mythical founding event of the United States, recent combat veterans have repeatedly been a profound political and often dissenting force in this nation. Few remember that during the War on Independence, entire regiments of the Continental Army mutinied in response to unpaid wages, unsanitary conditions, and wholly inadequate provisions, and that in one case General George Washington had no choice but to bow to their demands, whereas in another he saw fit to set an example by executing numerous mutineers.

In another instance, a small army of disgruntled "patriot" soldiers marched on the Continental Congress Hall in Philadelphia and surrounded and aimed cannons on it until the legislators agreed to pay them owed wages. Especially towards the end of that long, indecisive struggle, lots of combat veterans didn't cohere with the conventional patriotic image with which they were later imbued. Consider the words of twenty-six-year-old Yale graduate Lieutenant Ebenezer Huntington—who fought at Bunker Hill, Long Island, and later

Yorktown—in July 1780:

> The insults and neglects which the army have met with beggars all description . . . they can endure it no longer. I am in rags, have lain in the rain on the ground for 40 hours past, and only a junk of fresh beef and that without salt to dine on this day . . . I despise my countrymen. I wish I could say I was not born in America. I once gloried in it but am now ashamed of it.[57]

Nor did such exasperated, indignant veterans disappear from public life after the victory over Britain and their own mustering out of the army.

Just before the drafting and ratification of the Constitution, when the US was governed by the oft-forgotten and repeatedly denigrated first of its founding republican documents, the Articles of Confederation, a wounded, decorated Revolutionary War veteran, Daniel Shays, led a Massachusetts rebellion against state-level wealthy, elite financier interests. During the war, American soldiers were paid (if at all) in "Continental" currency, severely deflated paper bills that rarely rated a tenth of their face value in gold specie. That said, the Continental currency represented a promise, a gamble on future victory, even in the darkest, most hopeless days of a see-saw revolution. However, for the desperately indigent soldiers who gravitated to Washington's Army, futures—as today's Wall Street tycoons call them—mattered little. What they needed was to buy food and clothing and pay property taxes right then.

Desperate as they were, many brave soldiers sold off their nearly worthless "Continentals" to wealthy speculators (lucky enough to have ample hard specie currency on hand) at a fraction of the face value in exchange for pressingly needed gold. So after the war, when those very speculators dominated the new Massachusetts government and wrote a fresh constitution slanted towards the interests of those same financiers, and then had the gall to demand immediate back payment—in the hard currency that few rural farmers had—on property taxes, Shays and his many backers were quite literally up in arms. Indeed, Daniel Shays had exhausted all his options before deciding on outright rebellion. He'd even sold off the saber gifted to him—for battlefield heroics—by the famed French aristocratic, expatriate revolutionary the Marquis de Lafayette.

Though eventually suppressed, mostly bloodlessly, Shays's Rebellion, as it is known by historians, was an important dissenting event in the young republic. A large contingent of recent combat veterans stood with Shays against the established state government. So terrifying was the rebellion to elite interests, and polarizing among famous Founding Fathers, that George Washington and Thomas Jefferson held stunningly oppositional views of the affair. Washington was appalled by the impertinence of the rebels and wrote:

> The accounts which are published of the commotions . . . exhibit a melancholy proof of what our trans-Atlantic foe has predicted; and of another thing perhaps, which is still more to be regretted, and is yet more unaccountable, that mankind when left to themselves are unfit for their own Government. I am mortified beyond expression when I view

> the clouds that have spread over the brightest morn that ever dawned upon any Country.[58]

Jefferson, commenting from the safe distance of France, where he was serving as ambassador, submitted a wholly different assessment:

> The late rebellion in Massachusetts has given more alarm than I think it should have done . . . I hold that a little rebellion now and then is a good thing . . . as necessary in the political world as storms in the physical. Unsuccessful rebellions, indeed, generally establish the encroachments on the rights of the people which have produced them . . . it is medicine necessary for the sound health of government.[59]

It matters little which esteemed founder's assessment was ultimately correct. The takeaway is that as early as 1786, just three years after the official close of the Revolutionary War, American combat veterans were asserting themselves, dissenting against established governments and their policies. It is an old tradition, indeed.

A CENTURY AND A HALF LATER, AFTER A COUPLE OF MILLION Americans had deployed to Europe and fought a largely unnecessary war against Germany on behalf of the French and British—more than 116,000 of whom never came home—they were promised significant combat "bonuses" in recognition of their service in perhaps the most inhuman, brutal conflict ever waged among human beings. Most veterans were content to wait out the established interval before receipt of the committed benefits. Then the stock market crashed in 1929, and the Great Depression kicked off. At one point some 30 percent of Americans were unemployed, many of whom were jobless veterans of the First World War.

So it wasn't all that surprising when thousands of those veterans marched on Washington, DC, demanding early payment of their promised bonuses. They were desperate, indigent, and optionless; the pledged bonuses were their only hope. Some wore their faded uniforms and sported their combat decorations. The Bonus Army, as they were quickly dubbed, were quite popular and had the support of the majority of Americans. Nonetheless, President Herbert Hoover—though he'd made his name as a noted humanitarian who'd raised and shipped emergency aid to the occupied Belgian people during the previous war—wasn't about to give in to this anguished army of combat veterans. Instead, he called out the active-duty US Army to break up the distressed encampment of Doughboys[60]—the popular nickname for World War I soldiers—posthaste.

Who was there as part of the disgraceful mission to violently suppress this gathering of American heroes? Three illustrious West Point graduates who would achieve international fame as top generals in the Second World War: Douglas MacArthur, Dwight Eisenhower, and George Patton. Suffice it to say that soldiers with fixed bayonets, having fired CS gas into the crowd, charged the encampment, brutalizing veterans and burning all before them along the way. Two died, including a baby, and over a thousand Bonus Marchers were injured.[61] General Patton—then a mid-career major, later a hero of the Battle of the Bulge relief expedition in World War II—now has a statue outside the West Point library, but probably few cadets know about the instructions he gave to his cavalry troopers before they assaulted the Bonus Army veterans:

> If you must fire do a good job—a few casualties become martyrs, a large number an object lesson . . . . When a mob starts to move keep it on the run . . . . Use a bayonet to encourage its retreat. If they are running, a few good wounds in the buttocks will encourage them. If they resist, they must be killed.[62]

The Bonus Army affair had deeply frightened the president and the entire national security state. They emerged from that near-run event—one could argue that it might have catalyzed a veritable revolution—committed to the idea that such a display of lower-class veteran solidarity could never again be countenanced. This was part of the genesis of increased veterans' benefits in the wake of World War II. With more than ten million former service members being unleashed into civil society after 1945, the potential for veteran revolt on a scale that would have dwarfed that of the previous war was an unacceptable threat to power and hierarchy.

So the government bought off its veterans with modest—though well-deserved and ultimately economically sound—housing and education subsidies through the famed GI Bill. Furthermore, through the maintenance—for the first time in US history—of a large standing army and an exaggerated threat of the Soviet Union in the Cold War, it continued to fund a massive military-industrial complex and a permanent national security state, kept the booming war economy rolling, and avoided a feared new Great Depression. Predictably, there was no Bonus Army–type activism among the now-canonized "Greatest Generation" veterans.

As I used to tell my freshman cadets in US history class when the Bonus Army came up, it was not that I wanted them to forget all the heroics of MacArthur, Eisenhower, and Patton during the necessary war with the Nazis and Imperial Japan, but simply that when they daily passed the prominent statues of the three on campus, they'd at least consider the role of these "great men" in the shameful suppression of their own people—the veterans who'd risked all in the trenches of World War I.

One of the biggest and most vocal proponents of the Bonus Army veterans—he personally visited them in Washington, DC—was the most influential and popular (near-celebrity) antiwar military voice of his or any era: retired Marine Corps Major General Smedley Butler. He was an odd little man—five feet, nine inches tall and barely 140 pounds sopping wet—who rocked the lecture circuit and the nation itself. For all but a few activist insiders and scholars, Smedley Darlington Butler is now lost to history. Yet more than a century ago, this strange contradiction of a man became a national war hero celebrated in pulp adventure novels, and then within thirty years, he was one of this country's most prominent antiwar and anti-imperialist dissidents.

The son of an influential Congressman, raised in West Chester, Pennsylvania, and educated in Quaker pacifist schools, he served in nearly all of America's major and minor "Banana Wars" from 1898 to 1931. Wounded in combat and a rare recipient of two Medals of Honor, he retired as the youngest, most decorated major general in the Marines.

He was a teenaged officer and a certified hero during an international intervention in the 1900 Chinese Boxer Rebellion and later became a constabulary leader of the Haitian gendarme, the police chief of Philadelphia (while on an approved absence from the military), and a proponent of Marine Corps football. In more standard fashion, he served in battle as well as in what might today be labeled peacekeeping, counterinsurgency, or advise-and-assist missions in Cuba, China, the Philippines, Panama, Nicaragua, Mexico, Haiti, France, and, again, China. Although he showed early signs of skepticism about some of these imperial campaigns or, as they were sardonically called then by critics, "Dollar Diplomacy" operations—military campaigns waged on behalf of US corporate business interests—he remained the prototypical loyal Marine until he retired.

Only then did Smedley Butler change his tune radically and begin to blast the imperialist foreign policy and interventionist bullying in which he'd recently been a prominent participant. In 1933, during the Great Depression, he claimed in what became a classic memoir passage that "war is just a racket" and added: "I spent thirty-three years and four months in active military service . . . . And during that period, I spent most of my time being a high class muscle-man for Big Business, for Wall Street, and for the Bankers."

Seemingly overnight, the famous war hero had transformed himself into an equally acclaimed antiwar speaker and activist in a politically turbulent era. Those were uncommonly anti-interventionist years in which veterans and politicians alike promoted what for America were fringe ideas. This was, after all, the height of what later pro-war interventionists would pejoratively label American "isolationism."

Nonetheless, Butler must still be rated as unique, for that moment and certainly for our own, in his unapologetic amenability to left-wing domestic politics and materialist critiques of American militarism. In the last years of his life, he would face increasing criticism from his former admirer, President Franklin D. Roosevelt, from the military establishment, and from the interventionist press. This was particularly true after Adolf Hitler's Nazi Germany invaded Poland and, later, France. Given the severity of the Nazi threat to mankind, hindsight undoubtedly proved Butler's virulent opposition to US intervention in World War II wrong.

Nevertheless, the long-term erasure of his decade of antiwar and anti-imperialist activism and the assumption that all his assertions were irrelevant have been shown to be historically deeply misguided. In the wake of America's brief but bloody entry into the First World War, the skepticism of Butler and a significant part of an entire generation of veterans about intervention in a new European bloodbath should have been understandable. Above all, however, his critique of American militarism of an earlier imperial era in the Pacific and in Latin America remains prescient and all too timely today, especially coming from one of the most decorated and high-ranking general officers of his time.

Smedley Butler's Marine Corps and the military of his day were in certain ways different sorts of organization from today's highly professionalized armed forces. History rarely repeats itself, in a literal sense anyway. Still, there are some disturbing similarities among the careers of Butler and today's generation of American forever-war fighters. All of them served repeated tours of duty in mostly unsanctioned wars around the world. Butler's conflicts may have stretched west from

Haiti across the oceans to China, whereas today's generals mostly lead missions east from West Africa to Central Asia, but both sets of conflicts seemed perpetual in their day and were motivated by barely concealed economic and imperial interests.

Yet whereas this country's imperial campaigns of the first third of the twentieth century generated a Butler, the hyperinterventionism of the first decades of this century hasn't produced a single even faintly comparable figure. Not one. Zero. Zilch. Why that is matters greatly and illustrates much about the US military establishment and contemporary national culture, none of it particularly encouraging.

When Smedley Butler retired in 1931, he was one of just three Marine Corps major generals, holding a rank (just) below that of only the Marine commandant and the Army chief of staff. Today, despite the military counting about nine hundred generals and admirals currently serving on active duty, including twenty-four major generals in the Marine Corps alone, and with scores of flag officers retiring annually, not a single one has offered genuine public opposition to almost nineteen years of ill-advised, remarkably unsuccessful American wars. As for the most senior officers, the forty four-star generals and admirals whose vocal antimilitarism might make the biggest splash, there are actually more of them today than there were at the height of the Vietnam War, even though the active military as a whole is now about half the size it was then. But adulated as many of them are, not one qualifies as a public critic of today's failing wars.

Instead, the principle patriotic dissent against those terror wars has come from retired colonels, lieutenant colonels, and occasionally more junior officers (like me) and enlisted service members. Not that there are many of us either. I consider it disturbing, as should every concerned citizen, that I know just about every one of the retired military figures who has spoken out against America's forever wars. These are, almost to a man or woman, incredible people, true servants, but, like myself, they simply fail to garner the mainstream media attention or make the potential public splash of a vocally antiwar general replete with his star-studded bling.

Something must account for veteran dissenters seeming to top out at the level of colonel. Obviously, there are personal reasons why individual officers chose early retirement or didn't make general or admiral. Still, the system for selecting flag officers should raise at least a few questions when it comes to the lack of serious antiwar voices among retired commanders. In fact, a selection committee of top generals and admirals is appointed each year to choose the next colonels to earn their first star. And perhaps it is not too big a surprise to learn that, according to numerous reports, "the members of this board are inclined, if not explicitly motivated, to seek candidates in their own image—officers whose careers look like theirs."[63] At a minimal level, such a system is hardly built to foster free thinkers, and this, given America's wars, should be considered something of a disaster, as well as breed potential dissidents.

Consider it an irony of sorts that this system first received criticism in the current era of forever wars when General David Petraeus, then commanding the highly publicized surge in Iraq, had to leave that theater of war in 2007 to serve as the chair of the selection committee. The reason was that he wanted to ensure that a twice-passed-over colonel, a protégé of his—future Trump National Security Advisor H. R. McMaster—earned his star. It took an eleventh-hour intervention by America's most acclaimed general of the time to get new stars handed out to prominent colonels stonewalled until then by Cold War–bred flag officers because they were promoting different (but also strangely familiar) tactics in this country's wars. Imagine, then, how likely it would be for such a leadership system to produce genuine dissenters-with-stars of any serious sort, let alone a crew of future Smedley Butlers.

Behind this system lay the obsession of the American officer corps with "professionalization" after the Vietnam War debacle. This first manifested itself in a decision to ditch the citizen-soldier tradition, end the draft, and create a not-so-all-volunteer force. The elimination of conscription, as critics predicted at the time, created an ever-growing civil-military divide even as it increased public apathy regarding American wars by erasing whatever skin in the game most citizens had.

More than just helping to squelch civilian antiwar activism, though, the professionalization of the military in general and of the officer corps in particular ensured that any future Smedley Butlers would be left in the dust (or in retirement at the level of lieutenant colonel or colonel) by a system geared to producing faux warrior-monks like former Secretary of Defense James Mattis and the current chairman of the Joint Chiefs of Staff, Army General Mark Milley. The latter may speak gruffly and look like a man with a head of his own, but typically he's turned out to be just another yes-man for another war-power-hungry president.

As I write, one group of generals reportedly has it out for President Trump, but not because they're opposed to endless war. Instead, they reportedly think that The Donald doesn't "listen enough to military advice" on how to wage war forever and a day. Sadly enough, in the age of Trump (and, to be fair, Obama and Bush before him), as numerous polls demonstrate, the US military is the only public institution Americans still truly trust. Under the circumstances, how useful it would be to have a high-ranking, highly decorated, charismatic retired general in the Butler mold to galvanize an apathetic public around those forever wars of ours. Someone of his credibility, character, and candor is needed more than ever today. Unfortunately, this military generation is unlikely to produce such a figure. In retirement Butler himself boldly confessed that, "like all the members of the military profession, I never had a thought of my own until I left the service. My mental faculties remained in suspended animation while I obeyed the orders of higher-ups. This is typical." Today, generals don't seem to have a thought of their own even in retirement. And more's the pity.[64]

FINALLY, THOUGH IT IS HIGHLY UNLIKELY THAT A SENIOR, nationally famous retired general like Smedley will rise in modern times—and unsurprising that a similar figure didn't grow out of the Vietnam era—it remains important, finally, to consider the profound role of dissenting veterans (if usually lower-ranking ones) in the doomed Vietnam War, which, before the "war on terror," had some claim to having been America's longest-ever conflict. Frankly, it would be an exaggeration to assert, as some do, that the student-based antiwar movement—or that of late-stage GI resistance—was the preeminent reason that the US finally withdrew from that ludicrous war. The sad truth is that most Americans supported the Vietnam War way after the mission was hopeless and clearly immoral. Nonetheless, there was an important aspect of the end of that war that's been largely suppressed.

Late in the Vietnam conflict, significant numbers of American soldiers, many of them draftees, began to resist the war. By 1970, subversive underground GI newspapers began to proliferate. Furthermore, entire squads and platoons began to refuse to patrol, to place themselves in harm's way in a war that by that point was clearly unwinnable and unethical. Perhaps the most extreme behavior, not all that uncommon late in the war, was the regularity of "fragging"—the practice of lower enlisted soldiers rolling grenades into the tents of superior officers or otherwise assassinating them. Consider the statistics: in 1970 alone there were 209 documented incidences of fragging.[65] The army, totally unprepared for such overt manifestations of indiscipline, didn't even begin annotating instances of fragging until 1969. Nevertheless, the practice increased in regularity and severity as the war wound down. In the first eleven months of 1971, some 215 incidents resulted in 12 more deaths. As of July 1972, when the last American soldiers were leaving Vietnam, there had been 551 reported fragging incidents, killing 86 and injuring more than 700.[66]

Perhaps this extreme behavior was justified by the absurdity and immorality of the Vietnam War; empathy demands that one recognize the logic of such actions. But then again, the murder of fellow Americans, be they motivated officers or not, strikes this author as abhorrent. This much is certain: in the Vietnam War—maybe the last conflict in which this was true—antiwar veterans were a vital part of the dissenting movement. Veterans for Peace (VFP) and About Face: Veterans Against the War, originally called Iraq Veterans Against the War (IVAW), are two of the most prominent. I'm proud to be a part of this nascent movement. Nevertheless, VFP and About Face combined pale in comparison to the numbers, significance, and power of the Vietnam Veterans Against the War (VVAW) of the previous generation.

Undoubtedly, former Senator and Secretary of State John Kerry's finest hour was his own role in the VVAW movement, specifically his testimony before Congress in the famed "Winter Soldier Hearings." Whatever flip-flopping, Iraq War–supporting nonsense that later defined his political career, no one can take away the profound eloquence of Kerry's plea as a recent, decorated combat veteran on Capitol Hill in 1971. Before the Senate, he spoke the following erudite words:

> We are asking Americans to think about that because how do you ask a man to be the last man to die in Vietnam? How do you ask a man to be the last man to die for a mistake? . . . We are here in Washington to say that the problem of this war is not just a question of war and diplomacy. It is part and parcel of everything that we are trying as human beings to communicate to people in this country—the question of racism which is rampant in the military . . . in the use of free fire zones, harassment interdiction fire, search and destroy missions, the bombings, the torture of prisoners, all accepted policy by many units in South Vietnam. That is what we are trying to say. It is part and parcel of everything.[67]

Even a cursory glance at his record demonstrates that Kerry peaked in 1971. But that doesn't undo all the good he did and represented, and it doesn't erase the importance of Vietnam veterans in the antiwar movement, in the tradition of patriotic dissent.

Even if it didn't exactly bring the war machine in Vietnam to a grounding halt, the GI resistance of the era absolutely terrified the militarist powers that be in a variety of institutions: senior career military officers fearful for systemic discipline, commanders in chief from both major parties—Presidents Lyndon Johnson and Richard Nixon were both horrified by the antiwar movement—and corporate defense industry leaders worried deeply about the dissent within the military. In fact, that was part of the motivation to end the draft—a move that was supported by just about every powerful lobby in government: the army, the Pentagon, Congress, and the Oval Office. Most, however, had little idea of the long-term consequences of this Faustian bargain.

Since the establishment of the AVF, dissent *within* the military establishment has dissipated to such an extent as to seem irrelevant or even nonexistent. In an all-volunteer force, as mentioned, it is rather easy to discredit an active-duty or veteran dissenter: "Hey, you *volunteered*," many pro-war militarists will counter. Forget for a moment the inherent logical fallacy at the root of such invalidation; the point is that the ready parry is *effective*.[68] Furthermore, without mass, representative service in America's wars, today's recruits are simply—demographically and statistically—less prone to dissent in general. Most see the military as either a dutiful calling or a socialistic (though they'd hardly use the term) meal ticket replete with housing, health, and pecuniary benefits. Because ironically for a military full of Ron Paul[69] libertarians,[70] especially in the officer corps, who at least theoretically hate socialism, its members serve in the most socialist institution in the United States.[71]

Still, neither motivation is liable to generate antiwar dissenters. Indeed, though the vast majority of my West Point classmate friends still serving have long since recognized the hopelessness of contemporary wars, most obediently resign themselves to continued combat deployments—not any longer because they *believe* in the mission, but rather since they see it as a "job" to be done, a professional obligation first and foremost. Today, my former peers and dear friends remain ensconced in Afghanistan and Iraq or repeatedly deploy their units as a "show of force" to "counter" Russia in Eastern Europe. None of these interventions are particularly advisable or likely to succeed, yet my former fellow officers have mainly accepted that. They've long since stopped asking questions about their own role in perpetuating and enabling a counterproductive American inertia-driven warfare state. They are mainly apoplectic, tired, and resigned by this point. And who can blame them, after two decades straight of deployments to these quagmires? Most military professionals aren't exactly ripe for dissent or, as is necessary, for forming the vanguard of a revitalized antiwar movement.

Against all odds and institutional impediments, however, there are still a handful of important public military veteran dissenters, mostly retired, who remain in the arena. That I know nearly every single one personally and can count them on the fingers of both hands without the assistance of toes is undoubtedly a disconcerting indictment of the military wing of modern patriotic dissenters. Still, they exist. Andrew Bacevich was, I suppose, the first of the prominent post-9/11 "war on terror" skeptics. In that sense, he was an example, a motivator, and eventually a mentor to me and many other later-stage veteran dissenters.

The roll now includes other distinguished voices, such as Matt Hoh, who served as a marine and did two tours in Iraq before entering the State Department and then resigning from his post in opposition to Obama's failed surge in Afghanistan. Matt, a dear friend now, nearly drank himself to death and even planned out his own suicide at one time.[72] No one ever said the path of conscientious, patriotic dissent was easy. Retired Lieutenant Colonel Danny Davis, another colleague and now a friend, deployed four times—twice each to Iraq and Afghanistan—during a twenty-one-year career and then famously blew the whistle on the absurdity of the Afghan War upon his return from his final tour in 2012.[73] A classical Republican of an older mold, Danny even occasionally appears on the rather mainstream Fox News to criticize America's endless wars. Both Matt and Danny fit squarely within the long, storied tradition of veterans' patriotic dissent; nonetheless, few Americans have heard of either of them, which is a tragic disgrace.

What's more, there are still organized antiwar veteran groups on the scene to this day. I work with the big three. Veterans for Peace has been around since the early 1980s, and mostly consists of older Vietnam veterans. The newer, disturbingly small but vital About Face: Veterans Against the War (formerly Iraq Veterans Against the War) is in the vanguard of intersectional anti-imperial, antiracist, anticapitalist, and pro–indigenous peoples movements.[74] About Face refuses to restrict its protests to the singular cause of ending one or many discrete wars and opposes structural militarism, imperialism, and its inevitable outgrowths of racism and classism. They do incredible work given their relatively small numbers and regularly punch above their weight on the activism scene. For example, they had a prominent presence at the Standing Rock Reservation protests against the environmentally destructive Dakota Access Pipeline path through native land.[75]

Finally, the newest antiwar organization, one that has real legs and is rapidly growing, is BringOurTroopsHome.us, a Mountain West–based, decidedly conservative organization in the Ron Paul–Rand Paul libertarian mold that opposes contemporary American hyperintervention. While some on the traditional antiwar left have understandable doubts about this group, their existence is—from my perspective—highly valuable. Specifically, they demonstrate the long-standing but oft-eschewed natural budding alliance between the antiwar progressive left and the similarly minded libertarian right.

The two sides need not agree on health care, welfare, or what to do with the resultant "peace dividend" that a more modest foreign policy would create. Such domestic policy is an argument for another day. Both want America to "come home," as did the failed but inspirational 1972 presidential candidate (and World War II hero) George McGovern.[76] It is finally time for the two natural antiwar allies to set aside their domestic, ideological differences and unite—with, according to polls, most of the American people behind them—to alter US imperial policy.

Such is the not altogether hopeful state of affairs in the veterans' antiwar, anti-imperial movement. There are good people, for lack of a better term, in the nascent, admittedly struggling modern dissenting veteran tradition. Regardless and for what it's worth, the few of us who bother to care can console ourselves with the knowledge that we are indeed part of a prominent pantheon that has nearly always proved to be on the right side of history. And that, assuredly, is a suppressed history that demands a recounting—especially because of the powerful challenges to dissent that today's veterans and citizens face.

6.

Dissent is dangerous. For all the talk of free speech in America, time and again the US government has suppressed anything smacking of subversion, especially in times of war, through oppressive legislation and the tacit approval of "patriotic," chauvinistic vigilante justice. Nonetheless, for all their often-violent enforcement methods, the powers that be have never succeeded in extinguishing the long American tradition of dissent. Although it is undeniable that prominent antiwar dissenters have been oppressed—often imprisoned, occasionally lynched—these true patriots have laid down a foundation for future opposition. In the process, they've established a tradition, a series of repetitive commonalities in the long pantheon of dissenters.

First off, these brave folks have demonstrated the inherent value of challenging power and the prevailing status quo. Without them America wouldn't be able to point to its sizable anti-imperialist movement at the turn of the twentieth century or to its mass anti–Vietnam War protests as evidence that its society self-corrects and evolves. More importantly, antiwar activists throughout US history have—in hindsight—been repeatedly proven *right*. Which raises some counterfactuals, demonstrates the inherent contingency of human affairs, and shows that other paths *were* possible. For example, had

World War I—sans American intervention—ended in a German victory or, more likely, a stalemate, it is quite possible that Adolf Hitler and the Nazis (who built their popularity on dissatisfaction with the punitive peace settlement imposed on Germany in 1918–19) would never have ascended to power. In other words, World War I resistors in the US, had they prevailed, might have averted the even bloodier, catastrophic Second World War.[77]

Admittedly, when I dare postulate such counterfactuals, I open myself to charges of presentism, relativism, and reliance on hindsight. But the careful student of the past must reject such accusations for what they are: ahistorical and designed to undermine all dissent. The same may be said of the ubiquitous, popular, usually politically conservative claims that one cannot fairly critique the decisions and actions of past figures on the basis of the supposedly different values of the era in question. The notion that even the most abhorrent behavior—be it slaveholding, native genocide, or aggressive wars of conquest—cannot be fairly criticized by modern readers or scholars imbued with inherently divergent sets of values is dubious and dangerous thinking. On the contrary, the record shows that at every phase of American history there *were* prominent opponents of *all* of these policies—abolitionists, native defenders, anti-imperialists—some of whom were quite famous. Just as there were alternative paths for US policy across the centuries, there were also nonconformist, alternative value sets.

Relatedly, there is a well-worn platitude that "the victors write history." And there is much truth in this, if not always in the literal sense. Certainly until the mid-1960s, when historians finally began writing "bottom-up" monographs from the perspective of common folks and marginalized communities, this was largely the case within academia. Most American history before then was deeply grounded in pageantry patriotic triumphalism and national exceptionalism. Some have referred to such narratives as Great (white) Man History. These tracts papered over oppositional viewpoints, contested policy making, and the stories of dissenting "losers" in the crafting of foreign policy. As a result, clashing and antithetical points of view and alternative values were quietly but ominously erased with the stroke of a pen. Thus Lincoln, for example, became a one-dimensional figure—a wartime commander in chief and great emancipator—absent nuance and with scant mention of his earlier career as a decidedly *anti*war dissenter. Such is the profound power of the seemingly passive, bookish historian. He—and back then they were mostly "he"s—thereby ensured that President Lincoln would not serve as an example for the motivation of antiwar dissidents of future times, such as the Vietnam era.

However, in *this* story, this reflection on dissent, the voices of alternative patriots rise to the surface. While most history homes in on the "victors" of the policy and ethical battles in US foreign affairs and tells that tale in a linear, often deterministic manner, from another perspective the record demonstrates that those very consensus "winners" were, more often than not, *wrong*. Their policies regularly resulted in imperial expansion, human rights violations, countless unnecessary deaths, and the dilution of republican values and institutions. In *this* story it is repeatedly the "losers," the resistors, who actually had the true national interests and ethical standards at heart.

Still, far be it from me to give the reader the wrong impression. It must ultimately be said that, then and now, patriotic dissent as herein defined is exceedingly rare. Dissent is difficult and risky, and it requires rare levels of moral courage. And though veterans have often formed part of the core of brave dissidents, opposition from within the military—while far more common than often thought—remains scarce. This has been especially true in periods, such as today, when the US military was populated by volunteer professionals. Consider the uncomfortable truth that since 9/11, though they've been charged with waging one unwinnable, absurdist war after another, not a *single* senior general has resigned in protest of those ill-advised conflicts.[78]

Nor have politicians dissented quite as often, as vehemently, or for as principled reasons as one might hope. It is important to make a distinction between partisan and patriotic dissent among such figures. Time and again in America's flawed two-party system—not a framework particularly nurturing of principled dissent—the political opposition has failed to meaningfully change the course of the American imperial ship. Rather, mainstream party leaders, whether Whigs, Republicans, or Democrats, have been motivated far more by partisanship than principles. Their opposition to the policies of the party in power were more often than not propelled by political rancor or their visceral dislike of a particular president. For example, the Whigs—a now defunct party that essentially *formed* as an anti-Jacksonian coalition of otherwise differing interests—simply hated a popular president. Sound familiar? Indeed, the reflexive anti-Trumpism of today has much historical precedent and is not as unprecedented as many citizens, media personalities, and politicians seem to assume.

The problem is that though the Whigs occasionally took more humane and anti-imperial foreign policy positions, they were usually characterized by political caution when in the minority and by moral timidity when in power. Many Whigs screamed to the high heavens, rhetorically, over Andrew Jackson's despicable Indian removal policies, but once they got one of their own in the White House, they did nothing to meaningfully alter these practices.[79] Furthermore, even though it was plain that a later Democratic President, James K. Polk, had purposefully instigated and then deceptively sold a war of conquest with Mexico, no more than a dozen Whigs demonstrated enough political courage to vote against the congressional war declaration. They remembered well the fate of the once powerful Federalist Party, which, in large part due to its public opposition to the wildly unnecessary War of 1812, went extinct in shockingly rapid fashion.[80] It turns out that an antiwar position is rarely a political winner in American history.

Only after Mexican-American combat proved more protracted and murderous than expected—it was the most bloody, per capita, for American troops of any conflict before or since—did sitting and newly elected Whig lawmakers like Congressman Lincoln turn against the war in great numbers. They had hedged, waiting for the war to become unpopular and for a grassroots antiwar movement, probably America's first, to sprout, before they became latecomers to the opposition. What's more, none of this stopped the Whigs from successfully running a famous general and a political neophyte, Zachary Taylor, for the presidency in 1848. The Whigs, it seems, were far more politically calculating than principled peaceniks.

Something similar unfolded in the aftermath of the November 2006 congressional midterm elections. Though the Democrats captured both houses in a landslide in what was truly a negative referendum on the Iraq War, they quickly rolled over when President George

W. Bush defied popular sentiment and instead escalated a failing intervention. They rhetorically opposed Bush's "surge" strategy and asked some tough questions of the new war commander, General David Petraeus, during hearings on the Hill, but they never even seriously *considered* reigning in the president's war powers, or cutting funding for the hopeless occupation of Iraq. To do so, they (probably correctly) surmised, would have been political suicide. It was also the right thing to do. Today's Democrats, like the Whigs before them, took to heart the "lesson" of the antiwar Federalist Party. Theirs, too, was partisan rather than principled dissent.

Given the power and persuasiveness of my experience in the Iraq War and its profound impact on my life, let me expound in some detail on the sordid recent history of America's tragic involvement in the country. *This* was the story I first studied at length, painfully so, in my period of political and philosophical transition during the then-latest war there.

THE MODERN STATE OF IRAQ WAS AN UNNATURAL FABRICATION, a Western invention carved out from three distinct provinces of the defeated Ottoman Empire in the aftermath of World War I. One province was mainly Sunni Arab, another Shia Arab, the last Kurdish (mostly Sunni Muslim).

Following their standard divide-and-conquer playbook—whereby vulnerable minority groups were often empowered—the British imperialists installed a Sunni king, from the Hashemite family of the Arabian Peninsula, atop the Iraqi throne. Iraq's Sunnis, though only 20 percent of the total population, would rule for the next eighty-odd years. When local Iraqi, mostly Shia, citizens rejected this foreign, colonial imposition and rose in rebellion, they were brutally suppressed by the British Army and aerial bombings from its new air corps, recently tested on Europe's Western Front.

Still, the days of overt imperialism and of the British Empire itself were numbered, and soon after World War II the artificially constructed state of Iraq was independent. Coups, rebellions, and other convulsions inevitably followed. The monarchy was overthrown; socialists, fascists, and Islamists squared off; and by the 1970s—when the dust finally settled—a secular Sunni strongman, Saddam Hussein, and his brutal Baath Party ruled Iraq with an iron fist.

In 1980 in the near-immediate wake of the Islamic Revolution, Saddam unleashed just to his east, in Iran, a massive, aggressive, and illegal invasion of the Persian heartland. Around one million were killed, on both sides combined, in the world's bloodiest conventional war of the late twentieth century. Through it all, Uncle Sam unapologetically backed—and even provided key intelligence to—Saddam's unconscionable invasion. Indeed, especially ironically given what followed in 2003, then-President Ronald Reagan even sent one Donald Rumsfeld as a special envoy to Iraq in order to make nice with him.[81]

But Washington miscalculated, as it has so often done in US history. Reagan and his presidential successor, George H. W. Bush, thought they could control their man, Saddam, and they couldn't. Desperately in need of funds after the war and (predictably) bent on regional hegemony, Saddam invaded and quickly conquered his southern neighbor, the oil-rich former British protectorate of Kuwait, in August 1990. Suddenly, in a cynical policy about-face, Bush—and the compliant media—dubbed Saddam the new Hitler and not taking military action tantamount to 1930s-era appeasement of Nazi aggression.[82]

Saddam foolishly fought a lopsided conventional war that played to all of America's strengths and his own deep-seated weaknesses—using poorly employed, outmoded Soviet-style set-piece tactics the US military had trained against for decades. Perhaps two hundred thousand Iraqis were killed in the campaign, compared to around a hundred Americans, many of whom died in friendly-fire incidents. Unfortunately, in the euphoric triumphalism of the relatively bloodless victory—a win that President Bush proclaimed had "kicked" the supposedly defeatist "Vietnam syndrome" once and for all—the US military and the relevant politicians in Washington learned all the wrong lessons from what was dubbed the Persian Gulf War.

Many swiftly concluded that America's armed forces were invincible, and—with the Soviet Union's December 1991 collapse having eliminated the nation's only near-peer competitor—US military action could accomplish almost limitless goals the world over. A significant swath of neoconservative Republicans and even a substantial core of neoliberal Democrats began to see President Bush's restraint in deciding not to conquer Iraq and remove Saddam as weak, almost quaint. This powerful and amply funded lobby began to coalesce in militarist, even neo-imperialist think tanks—such as the Project for a New American Century (PNAC)—in Washington, DC, during the 1990s with two major goals in mind: finish the job in Iraq, then spread American power (and, for the sake of appearances, democracy) throughout the Middle East.

Bush would ultimately lose the 1992 election, but his successor, Bill Clinton, still surrounded Iraq with military bases and ships, imposed no-fly zones, bombed Iraq as often as once every three days, and imposed—throughout the 1990s—the strictest, most crippling economic sanctions regime in history. During that decade, some five hundred thousand Iraqi children died of sanctions-related malnutrition and preventable diseases. This was twice the number of civilians killed in the atomic bombings of Hiroshima and Nagasaki in August 1945.

Through it all, a special kind of American governmental callousness was prevalent. In 1996 President Bill Clinton's future secretary of state—who would be the first woman ever in the position—then–UN Ambassador Madeleine Albright, when asked in an interview on *60 Minutes* if, given the credible reports of half a million Iraqi deaths, the sanctions regime was worth the cost, she promptly answered, "I think that is a very hard choice, but the price, we think, the price is worth it."[83]

The pro–regime change coalition was so close to their dream and yet so far from it when the US Supreme Court declared George W. Bush, the son of the Gulf War commander in chief, president in 2001. The average American just didn't seem to have the stomach for deploying hundreds of thousands of ground troops and waging a war of choice. What was needed was a provocation, a pretense, a plausible justification for a final endgame invasion to remove Saddam. The PNAC crowd knew it, too. In a memo before the 2000 election, the organization recognized that a shift of US policy towards practical, war-induced Iraqi regime change would require "some catastrophic and catalyzing event, like a new Pearl Harbor."

Bush's foreign policy team—ten of the eighteen signatories of PNAC's original letter to President Clinton would eventually serve in his administration—manipulated a pliant, ill-informed president into an invasion of Iraq through the opportunistic exploitation of the fear and chaos that necessarily followed the unprecedented 9/11 attacks. This team constituted a veritable who's who of influential Bush officials: Vice President Dick Cheney, Secretary of Defense Donald Rumsfeld, Rumsfeld's trusted subordinates Paul Wolfowitz and Richard Perle, Deputy Secretary of State Richard Armitage; UN Ambassador (and future Trump National Security Adviser) John Bolton, and Special Assistant to the President for the Greater Middle East Zalmay Khalilzad, the future ambassador to both Iraq and Afghanistan.

Though senior US intelligence officials all concluded that Osama Bin Laden—whom the CIA had once also backed in his jihad against the Soviet occupation of Afghanistan in the 1980s—and his Afghan-based Al Qaeda terror outfit were behind the attacks, the PNAC alumni on Bush's team almost immediately pivoted to proposed military action against Iraq, in some cases while the Pentagon still smoldered.

Still, Bush felt he had to strike Afghanistan first. Public anger and outcry demanded it. Nonetheless, owing to equal parts incompetence and experimental military dogma, Bin Laden escaped to Pakistan in the ensuing joint CIA–Special Forces–Afghan warlords campaign. The Taliban was soundly defeated, of course, but, rather than maintain focus on mopping up Al Qaeda remnants, seriously grappling with the terrorist safe haven in the frenemy state of Pakistan, and/or investing heavily in Afghan reconstruction, Bush and company quickly turned their attention to the preferred PNAC-era target of choice: Saddam's Iraq.

Mountains of now available—and, truthfully, *then* available—evidence demonstrates a few salient, inconvenient, deeply disturbing truths about Bush's 2003 invasion and subsequent occupation of Iraq. First, the preponderance of senior administration officials, including, it seems, Bush, had decided on war long before requesting an Authorization for the Use of Military Force (AUMF) from Congress, and far earlier on than they dared admit publicly. Second, the Bush team at once fabricated, twisted, misinterpreted, and tactically leaked intelligence in order to manufacture and sell an outright invasion to the American people.[84] Then they lied about the whole thing—blatantly, repeatedly, and routinely. Most citizens and all but twenty-two US senators willingly went along for the ride. I'm embarrassed to say I was among them.

Particularly galling is the knowledge that the expertise on both Iraq and the region existed at the time. Not only these experts, oft-ignored by the Bushies as geeky wonks, but really anyone with a working knowledge of the basic contours of Islam, Mideast geopolitics, and the framework of the Iraqi state ought to have predicted (and many did) that overthrowing Saddam and imposing majoritarian democracy at the tip of the bayonet would catalyze mostly dormant ethno-sectarian divides and potentially kick off a civil war.

Not that the American president at the time knew or cared to know about any of this. His shocking lack of intellectual curiosity was such that credible reports indicate he didn't even know the difference between Shia and Sunni Islam in the run-up to the invasion.[85] Naturally, both of the predictable outcomes described above came to pass by early 2005. The civil war killed hundreds of thousands, conservatively, and perhaps up to a million Iraqis.[86] Some five thousand US troops died in combat, trapped between and attacked by the warring sides. Despite a temporary lull in violence during Bush and Petraeus's "surge" in 2007–10, the two sides never reconciled politically, and by 2013 the briefly dormant seeds of Sunni jihadism sprouted into the Islamic State (ISIS). That eschatological, apocalyptic Islamist nightmare had, in a final bit of irony, largely been birthed in US military prisons during the earlier phase of the war, and in 2014 it conquered huge swaths of Eastern Syria and Northern and Western Iraq. Soon enough the US military was back in Iraq, where it remains as of this writing.

Upon recounting this litany of sequential failure, I'm often left stuck on something highly disturbing that I heard from one Iraqi after another in 2006–7. Life was *better*, they'd tell me over tea in their humble homes, under Saddam. At least then there was security, no sectarian war, no religious police in the streets. Young men and women could dress however they liked, hold hands in the street, and drink alcohol in cafes along the Tigris River. There were no severed heads in the schoolyards, and there was no such thing as Al Qaeda within Iraq. Even downtrodden Shia, who hated Saddam with a passion, often told me this. We, the American Army, they concluded—though they never blamed me personally—had ushered in these dark days. And the days in Iraq are dark still. I left all those meetings with sadness, guilt, and regret in my heart. I left Iraq itself just after Christmas in 2007 with all those same feelings. They've never fully dissipated and I fear they never will.

Still, as I left Iraq with life and limbs intact, I dared dream that better times lay ahead. From the combat zone, I first vaguely and then carefully tracked the unlikely rise of a junior black-skinned Democratic Illinois senator with African-sounding first and last names and a middle name, Hussein, the same as the second name of the Iraqi dictator my army had been sent to topple. He ultimately bested the seemingly anointed front-runner in the primaries, Senator and former First Lady Hillary Clinton, largely on his vaguely anti–Iraq War speech of some five years before, when he was just a modest state senator without much to lose on the issue. Full disclosure: I secretly did a limited bit of canvassing for the man on both sides of the Ohio River while stationed at Fort Knox, Kentucky, and then voted for him in two consecutive presidential elections.

Barack Obama promised "hope and change," a refreshing (if ambiguous) alternative to the sins of the Bush years. The very abstractness of that slogan, however, allowed his supporters to project their own wants, needs, and preferred policies onto the future Obama experiment. So perhaps none of us ought to have been as surprised as many of us were when, despite slowly pulling troops out of Iraq, he only escalated the Afghan War, continued the forever wars in general (even returning to Iraq in 2014), and set his own perilous precedents along the way.

It was, after all, Obama who, as an alternative to large-scale military occupations, took Bush's drone program and ran with it. He would be the first president to truly earn the sobriquet "assassin in chief." He made selecting individuals for assassination in "Terror Tuesday" meetings at the White House banal and put his stamp of approval on the drone campaigns across significant parts of the planet that followed—even killing American citizens without due process. Encouraged by Secretary of State Hillary Clinton, he also launched a new regime-change war in Libya, turning that land into a failed state filled with terror groups, a decision that, he later admitted, added up to a "shit show." After vacillating for a couple of years, he also mired the US, however indirectly, in the Syrian civil war, empowering

Islamist factions there and worsening that already staggering humanitarian catastrophe.

In response to the sudden explosion of the Islamic State—an Al Qaeda offshoot first catalyzed by the Bush invasion of Iraq and actually formed in an American prison in that country—and its taking of key Iraqi cities and smashing of the American-trained Iraqi army, Obama loosed US air power on it and sent American troops back into that country. He also greatly expanded his predecessor's nascent military interventions across the African continent. There, too, the results were largely tragic and counterproductive as ethnic militias and Islamic terror groups spread widely and civil warfare exploded.

Finally, it was Obama who first sanctioned, supported, and enabled the Saudi terror bombing of Yemen, which, even now, remains perhaps the world's worst humanitarian disaster. So it is that, from Mali to Libya, from Syria to Afghanistan, every one of Bush's and Obama's military forays has sown further chaos, startling body counts, and increased rates of terrorism. It's those policies, those results, and the military toolbox that went with them that Donald J. Trump inherited in January 2017.[87] That for-me *lived* experience of war and political disenchantment led many concerned citizens towards a sense of apathy. This is understandable but, I assert, dangerous.

Admittedly, salvation of the national soul will not come from within the two-party system. That structure isn't *designed* to cultivate meaningful antiwar or anti-imperial dissent. It is little more than an arrangement for the polite rotation of political elites—and their wealthy special-interest backers—in and out of office every two, four, or eight years. The two-party system is not devised for serious structural change or for "turning" the big ship of state. House representatives serve only two-year terms and are thus continually running for reelection; the military budget is constitutionally mandated to be funded annually. Perhaps counterintuitively, these timelines inhibit major changes in American foreign and military policy. Absent term limits, the removal of big money from politics, or the growth of a mass-scale, grassroots antiwar citizens' movement, don't expect big things from what prevails in a Democratic or a Republican opposition in Washington.

As John Kenneth Galbraith noted, "groupthink" pervades American politics and almost all governmental institutions, thereby inhibiting principled dissent. He identified the practical and philosophical limitations of loyalty to the state and of working for change from within, or "inside," the system. As the famed economist and diplomat wrote in 1999,

> The man or woman who fully accepts the policy and has belief therein is known as a good soldier . . . . The administration of foreign policy thus comes very close to the enforcement of belief. Such commitment is never total; some of those involved manage to maintain their independence of thought. But in so doing, they risk being seen as unreliable—in the common State Department expression . . . they are not useful. The usual case, however, is acceptance. [A] consequence is that the requisite belief, once established, cannot easily be changed, perhaps not changed at all. One must be consistent in one's faith. One accepts the policy . . . however improbable.[88]

This may be particularly true, unfortunately, in the United States. Indeed, as one famous foreign observer of American political culture, Alexis de Tocqueville, wrote way back in the early nineteenth century, "I know of no country in which there is so little independence of mind and real freedom of discussion as in America."[89] That's quite an indictment from a citizen of a French monarchy. Dissent, especially of the antiwar and anti-imperial variety, is as hard as it is rare, and it must rise from the people, from the grassroots. Elite political leaders couldn't save the republic before, and they won't salvage it now.

Only a collective commitment to education followed by action has any real hope of excising the rot of militarist imperialism from the national soul. This demands, even requires, that no matter how dark the current days, the citizenry decidedly eschew apathy in favor of activism. Despite the economic insecurity and inherent business of most Americans' lives, the people have no choice—if they wish to save themselves or the republic—but to read, study, inform themselves about the venal US foreign policy that unfolds in their name. Then, this "woke" populace must demand—at the polls and on the streets—that not only America's military posture but also the pageantry patriotism that informs it be completely altered and redefined. If this sounds like a vague or idealistic call to arms, well, it is! It has historical precedent, and honestly, what other choice do we have?

Epilogue

I'm no dissenting hero. I didn't attend my first protest rally until I was thirty-two years old, and it wasn't even an antiwar event. Not directly, at least. I was a few years out of Afghanistan and teaching US history at West Point. Then, empire—as it always does—came home, this time in the form of increasingly militarized and Pentagon-equipped policing in neighborhoods of color across the nation. Thanks to YouTube and social media, pervasive instances of police brutality and the killing of unarmed, mostly young black men streamed into public consciousness.

It was all brought home to me when a black man, Eric Garner, was choked to death by a white New York City police officer on a troubled street corner in my home borough of Staten Island for the alleged crime of selling loose cigarettes. As a student of civil rights history, an aspirant activist, and the lead instructor (oddly enough) in African American history at West Point, I felt galvanized into action.

The result: I found myself teaching cadets by day, then changing into jeans and a hoodie and driving 90 minutes to Staten Island, protest sign in tow. There I would attend Eric Garner rallies and shout at the police. Hours later, I would trek back to the military academy, rinse and repeat. It felt good to be out on the streets, but of course it changed nothing. America's warrior cops still operate with near impunity, using US military counterinsurgency tactics (sometimes with Israeli Defense Force training) in communities of color as if they were occupied enemy territory.[90] Nevertheless, something clicked inside of me. I left these rallies feeling like a real *citizen* and, maybe for the first time, finally saw everything so clearly: the connection between endless war abroad and curtailed civil rights and liberties at home. How could I sit on the sidelines, obediently climb the army career ladder, and *not* rededicate my life to preserving all the good (that remains) in this ostensible, aspirational republic of ours? What followed was a long, circuitous journey that, for now, culminated with this book.

After leaving West Point, which was just as traumatic as getting there at first was thrilling, I embarked on what would become the second act of my life, though it wasn't clear to me at the time: being an activist. The "Lost Generation" novelist F. Scott Fitzgerald—also a World War I–era veteran, along with some of his disgruntled peers—wrote, "There are no second acts in American lives."[91] The remark was inserted without any context in an unpublished book, so it's difficult to know what the famed author of *The Great Gatsby* meant by it. Still, if I take it at its face value, I must respectfully disagree with this literary hero of mine. The play of my life, at least, now seems to be in the middle of a riveting second act. The seemingly always damp streets of Staten Island may have provided the setting for its opening scene, but what followed has been an expansive whirlwind journey that has spanned five years so far.

It started slow in 2017, when, as a student at the US Army's Command and General Staff College, I was studying formulaic, outmoded, and patently absurd doctrines for planning and executing everything from "limited" to "total" wars against politely renamed enemies that bore remarkable resemblance to the Russians, Chinese, and Iranians. That was by day. In the evenings, I breezed through ridiculously easy homework assignments and then—as has been the touchstone habit of my life—turned attention to my books. But now I began to translate what I read, highlighted, wrote, and thought into an increasingly prolific stream of critical articles for publication. At the outset, most of my work critiqued the conduct of America's hopeless wars; then I shifted to doubts about the efficacy of those conflicts and finally vehement opposition to the very justification and morality of these crusades.

What began as an article a month in 2017 quickly multiplied to one a week in 2018 and reached an average of eleven a month over the last two years. The range and readership of the publications also expanded. Soon enough, even while on active duty, I began to accept invitations (mostly over weekends) to give speeches and join conference panels. Two days a month on the road turned into four and now is typically eight to twelve. Radio, podcasts, and alternative video media interviews also became a regular feature of my life. By the time I medically retired in February 2019, the whole activist, antiwar lifestyle had become more than just a full-time gig—rather overwhelming.

Yet it felt important (perhaps a little self-important), gave me a sense of purpose, and, though far from a cure-all, kept at bay my emotional demons lurking—at least for now—just under the surface of polite daily life. Activism has been as demoralizing as it's been invigorating. Street rallying feels like active citizenship in the traditionalist sense, but it's also lonely—especially when the crowds are small—and, since so few positive outcomes seem to derive from doing what we call "the work," more than a bit dispiriting.

No matter; I, for one, am in it for the long haul. There was a time, not so long ago, when I didn't expect to make it to thirty. I'm thankful for the mornings these days, and I'm inspired by the folks around me in "the movement" who dare to care and choose what I call cultural collectivism over cultural capitalism. Fear not, this has little to do with economics or the Cold War. Rather, it is the decision of the activist to commit their limited surplus time to the good of the collective body of citizens, rather than the more popular construction—think Bush's "go shopping" counsel—which prioritizes the pledging of nearly all free time to personal or (nuclear) family satisfaction.

No, I'm not channeling (or half as smart as) Karl Marx, and this isn't a third-rate rehash of *The Communist Manifesto*. But if one sets emotion aside for a moment, thinks rationally, and is spiritually honest, one *must* conclusively discern that the three existential perils Americans face today—to their republic (endless war) and their survival (nuclear catastrophe and climate crisis)—can only be curtailed (and time is ever so short, folks[92]) through collectivist, face-to-face, I-am-my-neighbor's-keeper activism. It matters not whether the participants in my increasingly immodest call to action frame it through a liberal-or-conservative, religious-or-humanist, nationalist-or-globalist lens. Given the state of affairs in our country, still the world's most powerful and influential in this moment, what matters is pitching in—doing, however modestly, "the work." And that demands that today's tribal citizens quit seeking panaceas and pointing fingers at one man, no matter how coarse or abhorrent.

No, America's—and the world's—impending disaster has been a complex collective exercise in which *all* of us were long, if unwittingly, complicit. It has been a bipartisan enterprise and has, since the 9/11 attacks, been the project of three separate presidential administrations, Democratic and Republican. We the People, to invoke the uniquely empowering honorific bestowed on the citizenry in the Constitution's preamble, helped shepherd—through our apathy, ignorance, and illusion—these existential threats to the republic and the species to their currently acute state. So because we all bear responsibility, take hope in the fact that we do so *together*, as a connected collective. If we want all that we love to survive—lives and liberties alike—We the People must fight back and, for our sins, take back the words *citizenship*, *empathy*, and especially *patriotism*.

None of this is easy; dissent rarely is. The decision to do it, for the politician and especially for the soldier, is perilous and weighty. Deciding when it is appropriate or even morally obligatory to turn against the policies of one's government is a complex matter. As the famous "father" of political conservatism Edmund Burke wrote, "The speculative line of demarcation where obedience ought to end and resistance must begin is faint, obscure, and not easily definable."[93] Nevertheless, nineteen years into this nation's globe-spanning, counterproductive, hopeless wars and the resultant erosion of civil liberties at home, Burke's "speculative line" has long since been crossed.

So consider this little book one obscure combat veteran's clarion call, a desperate plea for his peers and the citizenry writ large to reframe their conceptions of dissent *as* patriotism and take action! For if not now, when? And if not a mass coalition of regular folks, civil and military alike, then who? There are no professional heroes waiting in the wings to intervene at the eleventh hour and save the world from climate change–induced extinction, catastrophic nuclear war, or the republic-destroying endless wars of our age. Regular folks across the racial, religious, political spectrum—veteran or not—are going to have to step up, take risks, and ante up for a revitalized movement defined by patriotic dissent. I for one know it's a service I'll be far prouder to someday tell my grandkids about than anything I did in combat. The best way to end these wars and the civil-military divide that permits them is to bridge the gap ourselves.

Acknowledgments

I had never planned to be a writer, certainly not as a profession. Hardcore combat grunt was the more appealing identity when my mother signed me into West Point and thus the army when I was all of seventeen years old. In retrospect, that was just a phase, albeit a long and deeply held posture. Like my earlier efforts to cultivate a streetwise veneer in the interest of that peculiar brand of 1990s Staten Island social acceptance, my insecurity-laden chauvinist patriotism actually masked a more cerebral core.

If living as a "double kid" was to be my lot, my most contented moments were always spent with the first love of my life: books. So even if, as I'm wont to claim, my writing career was accidental, leaving militarism behind and making a living largely with my library has felt like coming home.

I self-consciously detest conventions, as perhaps all aspiring artists purport to. Yet while my decidedly conventional list of influences and loved ones is bound to be incomplete, a few acknowledgments are in order. This book wouldn't have been possible without Steve Wasserman of Heyday and our meet-cute arranged by my great mentor and friend Bob Scheer. This project, and in a real sense the concept of patriotic dissent, flowed from the conversation that ensued that day in Los Angeles. Both men believed in this venture and sentiment with a passion that transcended the business end of the publishing world.

Steve took up the mantle—believed in me—and brought *Patriotic Dissent* to fruition. He handed me off to a staff, notably Emmerich Anklam and Gayle Wattawa, that guided the editorial process with competence and professionalism that should be the gold standard for the entire industry. All of them made this a far better book than it might otherwise have been.

I'd have never had the occasion to meet a legendary journalist like Bob, or a notable publisher like Steve, had someone in "the biz" not taken notice of the desperately unpolished musings of a disgruntled army officer. Tom Engelhardt published my first rant about the Muslim world's history and America's military tragedy therein years ago, though with the distinct caveat that I submit to substantial editing. Tom remains the most intense editor in the game, and he taught me more than anyone else about style, research, and finding one's true authorial voice. His trust also made me believe, for the first time, that I could be a real writer.

More than a little thanks is due to Andrew Bacevich. My old boss on the West Point Department of History faculty, retired Colonel Ty Seidule, assigned my cadet colloquium *The New American Militarism* back in 2005. It took courage to select such a text at the height of the Iraq War we students were all knowingly headed off to join within the year. Few books have challenged me so foundationally, and though I forgot about Andy for a number of combat-distracted years, by the outset of my writing career it's fair to say I was doing my own young Bacevich impression. I like to think I've grown since then and developed my own voice, but he will always be more of an influence and mentor than he'll ever know.

In the years since, I've written and worked for a variety of publications, ranging from the alt-left to the paleo-libertarian. My former colleagues and editors at *Truthdig*—beginning with Bob Scheer, and including Kasia Anderson, Jacob Sugarman, and the great Chris Hedges—personified the first kind of publication. Eric Garris and Scott Horton of *Antiwar.com* are equal parts bosses and friends, and Jacob Hornberger at the Future of Freedom Foundation has given me the space to be historical and verbosely analytical to my heart's content. Several of my arguments in this book grew out of articles I wrote for a few of these publications. Finally, the support, friendship, and activist example of Ben Cohen has been a genuine inspiration.

Teaching history back at the academy was the joy of my professional life. Retired Colonel Gregory Daddis was so much more than my immediate superior in the American History division. He modeled the truest form of the soldier-scholar and challenged my mind with tough academic and pedagogical concepts—and my palate with classy cocktails—on evenings I'll never forget. My colleagues in the department, notably Mark Bergman, Rory McGovern, Andy Forney, and Mark Ehlers, some of whom are still on active duty, made me a better teacher and human being on the daily.

Next, I must not forget those fierce yet gentle souls, my dear friends in the peace movement. I watched *Born on the Fourth of July* as a rather gung-ho youth, and I certainly never imagined I would someday share a stage and a friendship with a legend like Mr. Ron Kovic. His presence and example are always humbling. The peace activism calling can be a lonely one. Therefore, my colleagues and buddies in About Face and Veterans for Peace—Ryan Keen, Will Griffin, Chris "Henri" Henriksen, Keagan Rylee Miller, Brittany DeBarros, and so many others—have been especially vital. All of them teach me something new each day.

What we lacked in inherited wealth, my wonderful family made up for it with profound love, dedication to closeness, and life-shaping examples. I come from a world where one's uncles are like fathers, and cousins like siblings. Something has been lost, I fear, in a modern society that so often lacks the collective nurturing of the extended family. It was a great gift to be a part of one. My father and I are, on the surface, nothing alike. That much is hard to deny. Yet it is to him I owe any lingering sense of work ethic, duty, and responsibility—and probably much of my brains.

I have but one sibling, my dear sister Amy. She's been a far better sister than I a brother. Her remarkable professional success and loving contribution to the family—and her adorable handful of a daughter, my niece Molly—probably go more unnoticed than they should.

My mother remains closer to me than any other adult in this world. Our daily calls ground me, as they always have. No one loves so purely and unselfishly or brings me such fun and joy. There's no one in this life I'd rather be stuck in a foxhole or trapped in an elevator with; we'd certainly laugh our way through it all.

My first book was dedicated to my then-six-year-old son Alexander James Michael, "AJ," and his namesakes who died under my command in Iraq. He is nearly twelve now and growing into an intelligent and sensitive young man. I take intense, unvarnished pride in him, without (I hope) the taint of living vicariously through his athletic or other achievements. I hope that he continues to learn even more from, and teach more to, me as the years pass. Since that original book, Samuel Robert, "Sam," was born, and he is now three years' worth of passion and joy. He is a red-headed tornado of cuteness and kindness, and I just know he has so much good to offer to this troubled world. My boys are my world, but they wouldn't be half the wonder they are without their mothers, Erika and Kate. If I am, as I suspect, a much better guy to have a beer with than to be married to, I don't regret a moment with either of them. They are great mothers and women in their own right.

Lastly, I dedicate *this* book to the two people who most molded my own value system, which I hope is reflected on every page: my maternal grandparents, Mae and Joe "Bubsy" Peteley—the king and queen of Midland Beach, Staten Island, New York. For me they will always be simply "Mam" and "Pop." Some people live on in the imagination and shape those they touched even decades after they leave this world. Anyone who knows my family would identify my grandparents as such with ease.

Mam was a kind, thoughtful critical thinker with a knack for the most difficult of daily newspaper crossword puzzles. Had she been born in a more modern time, she might have taught college literature rather than serving, as she did, as a rather dignified and "aristocratic" working-class homemaker. Pop wore the requisite masculine credentials—and the actual medals—of a Greatest Generation World War II navy veteran and career NYC firefighter, but these trappings mostly just gave him the credibility to cry over every sad film and each and every move his beloved grandchildren made.

Pop died the summer before my academy graduation. He had told his doctor weeks before that he didn't mind dying so much, but he couldn't miss that ceremony. "Imagine," he'd repeatedly say, "someone from *our* family, *our* neighborhood going to West Point!" His was a pride without pretension, however. He didn't make it, but he *was* there, just as he joined me in Iraq and Afghanistan.

He and Mae knew tragedy, of course. They lost a son to drug addiction and watched another slowly destroy himself. I remember one evening, around middle school, when I decided to ask him about the blanket and pillow he kept stashed in the back seat of what I remember as his cigarette smoke–filled brown Datsun. Cars *were* stolen in our neck of the Island—my mother's only recently had been—so I had to query why he kept these items visible and absolutely never locked his car. Was it for my uncle, his troubled son Jack? "Yes," he replied, "but not just him." He told me, with what I now recognize as honesty in his eyes, that he would rather his car be stolen than for any of the occasional local homeless not to know they could find warmth, if necessary, in "Bubsy" Peteley's car. I think on that now and suppose, though it took many years to manifest, *that* was the moment I became a liberal.

Notes

1. "Monthly Civilian Deaths from Violence, 2003 Onwards," Iraq Body Count database, iraqbodycount.org/database.

2. Hendrik Hertzberg, "Cakewalk," *New Yorker*, April 7, 2003, newyorker .com/magazine/2003/04/14/cakewalk.

3. Victor Navasky and Christopher Cerf, "Who Said the War Would Pay for Itself? They Did!" *Nation*, March 31, 2008, thenation.com/article/archive /who-said-war-would-pay-itself-they-did.

4. Jesse Rifkin, "'Mission Accomplished' Was 12 Years Ago Today. What's Been The Cost Since Then?" *Huffington Post*, May 1, 2015, huffpost.com /entry/iraq-war-mission-accomplished_n_7191382.

5. "Fatalities by Year and Month, Iraq," icasualties.org.

6. Jane Mayer, "Donald Trump's Ghostwriter Tells All," *New Yorker*, July 18, 2016, newyorker.com/magazine/2016/07/25/donald-trumps -ghostwriter-tells-all.

7. Kurt Vonnegut, *A Man without a Country* (New York: Random House, 2005), 101–102.

8. Eric T. Dean Jr., "The Myth of the Troubled and Scorned Vietnam Veteran," *Journal of American Studies* 26, no. 1 (April 1992): 59–74.

9. Andrew J. Bacevich, *Breach of Trust: How Americans Failed Their Soldiers and Their Country* (New York: Henry Holt, 2013).

10. Justin Fox, "Telling Us to Go Shopping," *Time*, January 19, 2009, content.time.com/time/specials/packages/article/0,28804,1872229 _1872230_1872236,00.html.

11. Chuck Marr and Nathaniel Frentz, "Federal Income Taxes on Middle-Income Families Remain Near Historic Lows," Center for Budget and

Policy Priorities, April 15, 2014, cbpp.org/research/federal-income-taxes-on-middle-income-families-remain-near-historic-lows.

12. Caitlin Oprysko, "Gabbard Sues Hillary Clinton over 'Russian Asset' Smear," *Politico*, January 22, 2020, politico.com/news/2020/01/22/tulsi-gabbard-sues-hillary-clinton-over-russian-asset-smear-102074.

13. Scott Neuman, "Military Goals of 'Surge' Largely Met, Petraeus Says," National Public Radio, September 10, 2007, npr.org/2007/09/10/14288514/military-goals-of-surge-largely-met-petraeus-says. Not for US troops, of course. American deaths peaked in mid-2007, and that was the bloodiest year for the military. See "Fatalities by Year and Month, Iraq," icasualties.org.

14. Nick Turse, "The Terror Diaspora: The U.S. Military and the Unraveling of Africa," *TomDispatch*, June 18, 2013, tomdispatch.com/blog/175714/nick_turse_blowback_central.

15. Andrew J. Bacevich, "America: 'Indispensable Nation' No More," *American Conservative*, February 22, 2019, theamericanconservative.com/articles/america-indispensable-nation-no-more.

16. *Merriam-Webster*, s.v. "patriotism," merriam-webster.com/dictionary/patriotism.

17. *Merriam-Webster*, 1828 edition, s.v. "Patriotism," webstersdictionary1828.com/Dictionary/patriotism.

18. *Merriam-Webster*, s.v. "Nationalism," merriam-webster.com/dictionary/nationalism#h1.

19. C. Boyd Pfeiffer, "'Under God' Wasn't in the Original Pledge of Allegiance," *Baltimore Sun*, September 28, 2015, baltimoresun.com/opinion/op-ed/bs-ed-pledge-allegiance-20150928-story.html.

20. "History of 'In God We Trust,'" United States Department of the Treasury, March 8, 2011.

21. Russell Heimlich, "Small Share of Americans in Active Military Duty," Pew Research Center, May 23, 2012, pewresearch.org/fact-tank/2012/05/23/small-share-of-americans-in-active-military-duty.

22. Colman Andrews, "What Public Institution Do Americans Trust More

Than Any Other? Hint: It's Not the Media," *USA Today*, July 8, 2019, usatoday.com/story/money/2019/07/08/military-is-public-institution-americans-trust-most/39663793.

23. Nikki Wentling, "VA Reveals Its Veteran Suicide Statistic Included Active-Duty Troops," *Stars and Stripes*, June 20, 2018, stripes.com/news/us/va-reveals-its-veteran-suicide-statistic-included-active-duty-troops-1.533992.

24. Kaitlyn Schallhorn, "Niger Attack Leaves 4 US Soldiers Dead: What to Know," Fox News, May 10, 2018, foxnews.com/world/niger-attack-leaves-4-us-soldiers-dead-what-to-know.

25. Caitlin Oprysko, "Gabbard Sues Hillary Clinton over 'Russian Asset' Smear," *Politico*, January 22, 2020, politico.com/news/2020/01/22/tulsi-gabbard-sues-hillary-clinton-over-russian-asset-smear-102074.

26. David Mayers, *Dissenting Voices in America's Rise to Power* (Cambridge, MA: Cambridge University Press, 2007).

27. Official Proceedings of the Democratic National Convention Held in Chicago, Illinois, July 7, 8, 9, 10, and 11, 1896, (Logansport, Indiana, 1896), 226–234. Reprinted in The Annals of America, Vol. 12, 1895–1904: Populism, Imperialism, and Reform (Chicago: Encyclopedia Britannica, Inc., 1968), 100–105; accessed at historymatters.gmu.edu/d/5354.

28. Daniel A. Sjursen, "Martin Luther King's Revolutionary Dream Deferred," *Truthdig*, January 13, 2018, truthdig.com/articles/martin-luther-kings-revolutionary-dream-deferred.

29. Martin Luther King, Jr., "Beyond Vietnam," April 4, 1967, soundcloud.com/kinginstitute/vietnam-a-crisis-of-conscience; Afi-Odelia Scruggs, "Beyond Vietnam: The MLK Speech That Caused an Uproar," *USA Today*, January 13, 2017,"usatoday.com/story/news/nation-now/2017/01/13/martin-luther-king-jr-beyond-vietnam-speech/96501636.

30. Jane C. Timm, "Steve Scalise and Other Republicans' Anti-MLK Day Votes under Scrutiny," MSNBC, January 19, 2015, msnbc.com/msnbc/steve-scalise-and-eight-republicans-who-voted-against-mlk-day.

31. Francis X. Clines, "Reagan's Doubts on Dr. King Disclosed," *New York Times*, October 22, 1983, nytimes.com/1983/10/22/us/reagan-s-doubts-on-dr-king-disclosed.html.

32. Mayers, 97.

33. John C. Calhoun, "A Southern Senator Opposes the "All-Mexico" Plan," HERB: Resources for Teachers, accessed February 18, 2020, herb.ashp.cuny.edu/items/show/1273.

34. William Jennings Bryan, "The Paralyzing Influence of Imperialism," Official Proceedings of the Democratic National Convention Held in Kansas City, Mo., July 4, 5 and 6, 1900, Chicago, 1900, pp. 205–227; accessed at mtholyoke.edu/acad/intrel/bryan.htm.

35. Daniel A. Sjursen, "The Long Shadow of World War I and America's War on Dissent, Part 1," The Future of Freedom Foundation, December 1, 2019, fff.org/explore-freedom/article/the-long-shadow-of-world-war-i-and-americas-war-on-dissent-part-1.

36. Andrew J. Bacevich, Faculty Biography, Department of History, Boston University, bu.edu/history/people/emeritus-faculty/andrew-j-bacevich.

37. Isaac Chotiner, "Andrew Bacevich on US Foreign-Policy Mistakes," *New Yorker*, January 13, 2020, newyorker.com/news/q-and-a/andrew-bacevich-on-foreign-policy-mistakes.

38. Ibid.

39. Daniel A. Sjursen, "American History for Truthdiggers: The Forgotten and Peculiar War of 1812," *Truthdig*, June 30, 2018, truthdig.com/articles/american-history-for-truthdiggers-the-forgotten-and-peculiar-war-of-1812.

40. Ibid.

41. Mayers, 47–48.

42. Mayers, 101.

43. Daniel A. Sjursen, "American History for Truthdiggers: Tragic Dawn of Overseas Imperialism," *Truthdig*, November 10, 2018, truthdig.com/articles/american-history-for-truthdiggers-tragic-dawn-of-overseas-imperialism, Stephen Kinzer, *The True Flag: Theodore Roosevelt, Mark Twain, and the Birth of American Empire* (2017), and Jackson Lears, *Rebirth of a Nation: The Making of Modern America, 1877–1920* (2009).

44. Andrew Bacevich, *The Age of Illusions: How America Squandered its Cold War Victory* (New York: Metropolitan Books, 2020): 38–41.

45. Daniel A. Sjursen, "American History for Truthdiggers: Tragic Dawn."

46. Ibid.

47. Sjursen, "Long Shadow."

48. Michael C. C. Adams, *The Best War Ever: America and World War II* (Baltimore: Johns Hopkins University Press, 1993).

49. Daniel A. Sjursen, "The Impeachment Show: Asking All the Wrong Questions on Ukraine," *Antiwar.com*, January 27, 2020, original.antiwar.com/danny_sjursen/2020/01/26/the-impeachment-show-asking-all-the-wrong-questions-on-ukraine.

50. Ken Hughes, "'Take on the F**king Demonstrators': Nixon, Vietnam and the Politics of Polarization," *Salon*, September 27, 2017, salon.com/2017/09/27/take-on-the-fing-demonstrators-nixon-vietnam-and-the-politics-of-polarization.

51. Dennis Laich, *Skin in the Game: Poor Kids and Patriots* (iUniverse, 2013).

52. Daniel A. Sjursen, "Niger, America's Forgotten Soldiers and Another Nameless War," *Hill*, October 6, 2017, thehill.com/opinion/national-security/354281-niger-americas-forgotten-soldiers-and-another-nameless-war.

53. "U.S. and Allied Wounded," Costs of War Project, Brown University, Watson Institute for International and Public Affairs, watson.brown.edu/costsofwar/costs/human/military/wounded.

54. Daniel A. Sjursen, "Was Ending the Draft a Grave Mistake?" *Truthdig*, April 3, 2019, truthdig.com/articles/was-ending-the-draft-a-grave-mistake.

55. Dennis Laich and Lawrence Wilkerson, "The Deep Unfairness of America's All-Volunteer Force," *American Conservative*, October 16, 2017, theamericanconservative.com/articles/the-deep-unfairness-of-americas-all-volunteer-force.

56. Daniel A. Sjursen, "The 'Adults' in the Room Are the Problem," *Nation*, December 27, 2018, thenation.com/article/archive/the-adults-in-the-room-are-the-problem.

57. Ebenezer Huntington, "Letters of Ebenezer Huntington, 1774–1781," *American Historical Review* 5, no. 4 (1900): 702–29, accessed at jstor.org/stable/1832776.

58. George Washington to Henry Lee, Oct. 31st, 1786, The George Washington Papers at the Library of Congress, accessed at shaysrebellion.stcc .edu/shaysapp/person.do?shortName=george_washington.

59. Thomas Jefferson to James Madison, December 20, 1787, Thomas Jefferson Papers, Series 1, General Correspondence, Library of Congress, accessed at shaysrebellion.stcc.edu/shaysapp/person.do?shortName =thomas_jefferson.

60. "Doughboys and the Birth of the Modern American Army," National World War I Museum and Memorial, theworldwar.org/doughboys.

61. Paul Dickson, *The Bonus Army: An American Epic* (New York: Walker & Company, 2004).

62. Ibid., 139.

63. Fred Kaplan, "Promoting Innovation," *Slate*, November 21, 2007, slate .com/news-and-politics/2007/11/army-to-petraeus-fix-us.html.

64. Daniel A. Sjursen, "Tomgram: Danny Sjursen, Why No Retired Generals Oppose America's Forever Wars," *TomDispatch*, February 20, 2020, tomdispatch.com/authors/dannysjursen/index.php?pos=1; Hans Schmidt, *Maverick Marine: General Smedley D. Butler and the Contradictions of American Military History* (Lexington: University of Kentucky Press, 1998).

65. Peter Brush, "The Hard Truth About Fragging," HistoryNet, historynet.com/the-hard-truth-about-fragging.htm.

66. Ibid.

67. John Kerry, Statement before the Senate Foreign Relations Committee, April 22, 1971, accessed from "Transcript: Kerry Testifies Before Senate Panel, 1971," National Public Radio, April 25, 2006, npr.org/templates /story/story.php?storyId=3875422.

68. Gregory A. Daddis, "'Patriotic' Veterans Only, Please," History News Network, February 16, 2020, hnn.us/article/174320.

69. Adam Weinstein, "Why Does the Military Love Ron Paul?" *Mother Jones*, February 24, 2012, motherjones.com/politics/2012/02/ron-paul -military.

70. George R. Altman and Leo Shane III, "Libertarians and independents are eroding the GOP's military support," *Military Times*, September 23, 2016, militarytimes.com/news/2016/09/23/libertarians-and-independents-are-eroding-the-gop-s-military-support.

71. Liesel Kershul, "The US Military Is a Socialist Organization," *Nation*, November 4, 2019, thenation.com/article/archive/socialism-united-states-military.

72. Matthew Hoh, Biography, Senior Fellow, Center for International Policy, internationalpolicy.org/matthew-hoh.

73. Tim Mak, "Award for Afghan war whistleblower," *Politico*, April 23, 2012, politico.com/story/2012/04/award-for-afghan-war-whistleblower-075516.

74. Official Website, About Face: Veterans Against the War, aboutfaceveterans.org.

75. Corey McGrath, "A Poor People's Resistance to War and Militarism," New York State Poor People's Campaign, January 28, 2020, poorpeoplescampaign.org/update/a-poor-peoples-resistance-to-war-and-militarism.

76. John Nichols, "The Genius of McGovern's 'Come Home, America' Vision," *Nation*, October 19, 2012, thenation.com/article/archive/genius-mcgoverns-come-home-america-vision.

77. Sjursen, "Long Shadow."

78. Daniel A. Sjursen, "The Generals Won't Save Us from the Next War," *American Conservative*, June 10, 2019, theamericanconservative.com/articles/the-generals-wont-save-us-from-the-next-war.

79. Mayers, 105.

80. Daniel A. Sjursen, "American History for Truthdiggers: The Fraudulent Mexican-American War (1846–48)," *Truthdig*, August 18, 2018, truthdig.com/articles/american-history-for-truthdiggers-the-fraudulent-mexican-american-war-1846-48.

81. Mike Pesca, "The Picture of Rumsfeld and Saddam," heard on "Day to Day," National Public Radio, December 19, 2003, npr.org/templates/story

/story.php?storyId=1554451.

82. Christopher Layne, "Why the Gulf War Was Not in the National Interest," *Atlantic Monthly*, Volume 268, No. 1; pages 55, 65–81, accessed at theatlantic.com/past/docs/unbound/flashbks/saudiara/layne.htm.

83. Sheldon Richman, "Albright 'Apologizes,'" Future of Freedom Foundation, November 7, 2003, fff.org/explore-freedom/article/albright-apologizes.

84. Jonathan Stein and Tim Dickinson, "Lie by Lie: A Timeline of How We Got Into Iraq," *Mother Jones*, September/October 2006 Issue, motherjones.com/politics/2011/12/leadup-iraq-war-timeline.

85. Tim Dickinson, "Bush's Islamic Ignorance," *Rolling Stone*, August 4, 2006, rollingstone.com/politics/politics-news/bushs-islamic-ignorance-88699.

86. Medea Benjamin and Nicolas J. S. Davies, "The Staggering Death Toll in Iraq," *Salon*, March 19, 2018, salon.com/2018/03/19/the-staggering-death-toll-in-iraq_partner.

87. Daniel A. Sjursen, "Tomgram: Danny Sjursen, Mad Policies for a Mad World," *TomDispatch*, January 23, 2020, tomdispatch.com/blog/176654/tomgram%3A_danny_sjursen%2C_mad_policies_for_a_mad_world_.

88. Mayers, 322–323.

89. Ibid.

90. Daniel A. Sjursen, "Tomgram: Danny Sjursen, Living at War (Forever)," *TomDispatch*, September 22, 2019, tomdispatch.com/blog/176607/tomgram%3A_danny_sjursen%2C_living_at_war_%28forever%29_.

91. Kirk Curnutt, interview, "All Things Considered," National Public Radio, May 8, 2013, npr.org/2013/05/08/182337919/fitzgerald-might-disagree-with-his-no-second-acts-line.

92. Danny Sjursen, "Humanity is Riding Delusion to Extinction," *Truthdig*, December 02, 2019, truthdig.com/articles/humanity-is-riding-delusion-to-extinction.

93. Mayers, 55.

About the Author

Daniel A. Sjursen is a retired US Army major and a contributing editor at *Antiwar.com*. His work has also appeared in the *New York Times*, the *Los Angeles Times*, *Salon*, the *Nation*, *Truthdig*, *TomDispatch*, the *Huffington Post*, and the *Hill*, among other publications. He served combat tours with reconnaissance units in Iraq and Afghanistan and later taught history at his alma mater, West Point. He is the author of a memoir and critical analysis of the Iraq War, *Ghost Riders of Baghdad: Soldiers, Civilians, and the Myth of the Surge*. He cohosts the progressive veterans' podcast *Fortress on a Hill*. He lives in Lawrence, Kansas. Follow him on Twitter at @SkepticalVet.